New Directions for
Teaching and Learning

Marilla D. Svinicki
EDITOR-IN-CHIEF

Improving the Climate for Undergraduate Teaching and Learning in STEM Fields

Roger G. Baldwin

EDITOR

Number 117 • Spring 2009
Jossey-Bass
San Francisco

IMPROVING THE CLIMATE FOR UNDERGRADUATE TEACHING AND LEARNING
IN STEM FIELDS
Roger G. Baldwin (ed.)
New Directions for Teaching and Learning, no. 117
Marilla D. Svinicki, Editor-in-Chief

Microfilm copies of issues and articles are available in 16mm and 35mm, as well as microfiche in 105mm, through University Microfilms, Inc., 300 North Zeeb Road, Ann Arbor, Michigan 48106-1346.

NEW DIRECTIONS FOR TEACHING AND LEARNING (ISSN 0271-0633, electronic ISSN 1536-0768) is part of The Jossey-Bass Higher and Adult Education Series and is published quarterly by Wiley Subscription Services, Inc., A Wiley Company, at Jossey-Bass, 989 Market Street, San Francisco, California 94103-1741. Periodicals postage paid at San Francisco, California, and at additional mailing offices. POSTMASTER: Send address changes to New Directions for Teaching and Learning, Jossey-Bass, 989 Market Street, San Francisco, California 94103-1741.

New Directions for Teaching and Learning is indexed in CIJE: Current Index to Journals in Education (ERIC), Contents Pages in Education (T&F), Current Abstracts (EBSCO), Educational Research Abstracts Online (T&F), ERIC Database (Education Resources Information Center), Higher Education Abstracts (Claremont Graduate University), and SCOPUS (Elsevier).

SUBSCRIPTIONS cost $89 for individuals and $228 for institutions, agencies, and libraries in the United States. Prices subject to change. See order form at end of book.

EDITORIAL CORRESPONDENCE should be sent to the editor-in-chief, Marilla D. Svinicki, Department of Educational Psychology, University of Texas at Austin, One University Station, D5800, Austin, TX 78712.

www.josseybass.com

CONTENTS

FROM THE SERIES EDITOR

About This Publication. Since 1980, *New Directions for Teaching and Learning* (NDTL) has brought a unique blend of theory, research, and practice to leaders in postsecondary education. NDTL sourcebooks strive not only for solid substance but also for timeliness, compactness, and accessibility.

The series has four goals: to inform readers about current and future directions in teaching and learning in postsecondary education, to illuminate the context that shapes these new directions, to illustrate these new directions through examples from real settings, and to propose ways in which these new directions can be incorporated into still other settings.

This publication reflects the view that teaching deserves respect as a high form of scholarship. We believe that significant scholarship is conducted not only by researchers who report results of empirical investigations but also by practitioners who share disciplines reflections about teaching. Contributors to NDTL approach questions of teaching and learning as seriously as they approach substantive questions in their own disciplines, and they deal not only with pedagogical issues but also with the intellectual and social context in which these issues arise. Authors deal on the one hand with theory and research and on the other with practice, and they translate from research and theory to practice and back again.

About This Volume. The STEM (science, technological, engineering, and mathematics) disciplines are leading the way in the reform of undergraduate education under the auspices of several national programs. This issue of NDTL chronicles the processes, successes, and insights of one of these major reform efforts.

Marilla D. Svinicki
Editor-in-Chief

MARILLA D. SVINICKI is the director of the Center for Teaching Effectiveness at the University of Texas at Austin.

PREFACE

The call for a more scientifically literate society is a constant drumbeat coming from the mainstream media and from reports of concerned organizations like the National Academy of Sciences. Typically enhanced STEM (science, technology, engineering, and mathematics) education, from elementary grades through life-long learning, is at the core of proposed solutions to this major national problem. This volume focuses on the role of higher education in confronting this national mission and cause.

Over recent decades, the United States has made a huge investment in understanding how to enhance student learning in STEM fields. Nonetheless, there can be little doubt that there is still a major disconnect between our knowledge of how to optimize student learning and the actual learning experiences that STEM faculty provide for most STEM undergraduates. Enhancing undergraduate learning is a duty of the national STEM faculty, but the responsibility is much more broadly distributed. Many stakeholders, including academic leaders, disciplinary organizations, and funding agencies, have important roles to play in the process of improving STEM teaching and learning in higher education.

This volume was conceived during conversations within the Center for the Integration of Research, Teaching and Learning (CIRTL) on how best to prepare future STEM faculty. (Note that CIRTL defines STEM as the natural and social sciences, technology, engineering, and mathematics.) CIRTL is one of two National Science Foundation Centers for Learning and Teaching focusing on higher education. The mission of CIRTL is to develop a national STEM faculty committed to implementing and advancing effective teaching practices for diverse student audiences as part of their professional careers. CIRTL seeks to prepare STEM graduate students and postdoctoral researchers to be both excellent researchers and excellent teachers.

The graduate schools of research universities are a critical leverage point for the improvement of national STEM education. Graduate students, 80 percent of whom are trained at only 125 research universities, flow into the STEM faculties of more than four thousand research universities, comprehensive universities, liberal arts colleges, and community colleges. Ironically, the research universities housing these graduate schools are the institutions of higher education whose missions most tend to draw faculty attention away from teaching. The most successful future faculty preparation programs tackle this challenge head-on by

demonstrating that achieving excellent research and excellent teaching is far more aligned than traditionally recognized. In CIRTL this concept is called teaching-as-research; Handelsman et al. (2004) call a similar idea scientific teaching.

However improved the preparation of future faculty in advance of their first faculty positions becomes, this national investment will be for naught if the institutional environments and disciplinary cultures in which STEM faculty find themselves do not continue to foster the advancement of their teaching. This volume acknowledges these climate issues and considers how to improve the climate for undergraduate teaching and learning in STEM fields across all institutions of higher education. Ideally, stakeholders at all levels (individual, departmental, disciplinary, institutional, state, and national) must work to improve conditions for teaching and learning in STEM and coordinate their efforts in support of the national STEM faculty.

The role of federal funding agencies has been and will continue to be central. Particularly important to elevating the attention to quality STEM education has been the National Science Foundation's (NSF) broader impact criterion. While broad impact was part of the original NSF charter, this recent emphasis in policy began with the *Shaping the Future* report, which suggested research directorates should expand resources for educational activities that integrate education and research. Critically, this call to action was targeted directly to the NSF STEM research directorates, in contrast to this mission being assigned only to the Education and Human Resources Directorate from which STEM educational funding traditionally derived. In association with this evolution in policy came an array of programs providing funding incentives to STEM researchers who aligned themselves with this policy. Most notable among these was the NSF CAREER Award for junior STEM faculty that requires proposers to develop innovative plans of work in both research and education. Recently the National Institutes of Health has been moving in a similar direction in its training grant programs and requirements for enhanced professional development of the many postdoctoral researchers that it funds.

STEM disciplinary societies also can play important roles in the effort to improve STEM undergraduate education. Academic departments, institutions, and funding agencies are remarkably insular, which is a major inefficiency and impediment for broad national change. Disciplinary societies have the potential to be powerful connection points fostering change across higher education. They can also play a key role in supporting the higher education initiatives of federal funding agencies as the societies interact with Congress and executive offices.

You will find the chapters in this volume to be insightful and inspiring. I am confident that *Improving the Climate for Undergraduate Teaching and Learning in STEM* will make an important contribution to the national dia-

NEW DIRECTIONS FOR TEACHING AND LEARNING • DOI: 10.1002/tl

logue on strategies for promoting high-quality undergraduate education in STEM fields.

Robert D. Mathieu

References

Handelsman, J., Ebert-May, D., Beichner, R., Bruns, P., Chang, A., DeHaan, R., Gentile, J., Lauffer, S., Stewart, J., Tilghman, S. M., and Wood, W. B. "Scientific Teaching." *Science,* 2004, *302*(23), 521-522.

National Science Foundation. *Shaping the Future: New Expectations for Undergraduate Education in Science, Mathematics, Engineering, and Technology.* Arlington, Va.: National Science Foundation, 1996.

ROBERT D. MATHIEU *is professor and chair of Astronomy at the University of Wisconsin–Madison. He also directs the Center for the Integration of Research, Teaching and Learning.*

NEW DIRECTIONS FOR TEACHING AND LEARNING • DOI: 10.1002/tl

Editor's Notes

The quality of undergraduate education in STEM fields (science, technology, engineering, and mathematics) has been a national concern for many years. Numerous organizations such as the National Research Council and the National Science Foundation have published multiple reports detailing the problems with standard approaches to educating college students. In a nutshell, these reports criticize the widespread use of large, lecture-based classes where STEM students sit passively and memorize large quantities of information they may never fully understand or know how to apply. These reports argue that traditional approaches to educating undergraduates in STEM fields are not adequate to prepare highly skilled workers for a science- and technology-based economy.

After such a vigorous and long-term effort to strengthen undergraduate STEM education, it is both surprising and discouraging that we continue to hear many of the same criticisms of STEM education raised in reports published one or two decades ago. And those calls to action and formulas for change sound remarkably similar to what thoughtful critics advocated long ago.

In the first decade of the twenty-first century, the calls for reform in STEM education are increasingly urgent. Our fast-paced global economy and concerns about terrorism, climate change, environmental pollution, worldwide epidemics, and other issues clearly demonstrate the need for scientifically literate citizens to address complex science-related issues with public policy implications. In addition, our knowledge-based economy requires workers with strong science, mathematics, and technology skills.

Although calls for STEM undergraduate reform have been loud and frequent, the response to these calls at the classroom and curriculum levels has been disappointing. In spite of vigorous discussion by national organizations and institution leaders, many STEM classrooms operate much as they did decades before. A graduate returning to campus twenty years after graduation might see little change in classroom procedures if he or she dropped in on an introductory chemistry or biology class.

Evidence suggests that the climate for enhancing teaching and learning in STEM fields remains less than favorable. A host of factors, detailed in the chapters that follow, prevent well-meaning professors from investing the time and creative energy in their teaching that is necessary to make STEM classrooms more welcoming to diverse students and to enhance the learning of all students who can benefit from a knowledge base in the sciences and mathematics. The chapters in this volume make clear that improving

NEW DIRECTIONS FOR TEACHING AND LEARNING, no. 117, Spring 2009   © Wiley Periodicals, Inc.
Published online in Wiley InterScience (www.interscience.wiley.com) • DOI: 10.1002/tl.339

the environment for undergraduate teaching and learning in STEM fields must be addressed at many levels (classroom, department, institution, state, and national) by the multiple stakeholders who recognize the importance of enhancing STEM education. The chapter authors examine the current climate for undergraduate education in STEM fields from varied perspectives. Each contributes to a realistic appraisal of the state of undergraduate STEM education. Each chapter identifies and explains concrete ideas and actions that can help to improve the climate for reforming STEM education at the college level.

Chapter One reviews the context for undergraduate teaching and learning in STEM. He examines the forces that are making STEM undergraduate education a priority concern as well as the powerful forces in the academic and STEM cultures that make educational improvement a challenging task. Baldwin considers how concerned stakeholders at many levels will need to work cooperatively and forcefully to make the STEM culture and climate more receptive to efforts to improve undergraduate education.

In Chapter Two, Karl A. Smith, Tameka Clarke Douglas, and Monica F. Cox discuss strategies for creating supportive learning environments in STEM classrooms and laboratories. Employing the How People Learn framework and backward design process, they illustrate the types of favorable environments that are conducive to learning in STEM. Essentially this chapter identifies ideal learning conditions that STEM educators should be working to provide for their students.

Brian P. Coppola considers in Chapter Three how to enhance STEM teaching and learning within the constraints imposed by competing faculty roles and responsibilities. He advocates creating teaching groups based on the proven model of research groups that are used in virtually all STEM fields. Coppola believes that this strategy can be used to monitor and improve teaching and learning in STEM classes while also helping to prepare STEM graduate students for their roles as educators.

Chapter Four provides the perspective of an academic administrator on how to create favorable conditions for enhancing STEM undergraduate education. Based on their experience in the College of Engineering at Penn State University, Thomas A. Litzinger, Richard J. Koubek, and David N. Wormley discuss strategies at the college, department, and individual faculty levels for facilitating educational reform. They briefly summarize reform efforts at these three important levels and share concrete and practical lessons learned that can be applied in other STEM education settings.

Chapter Five puts specific STEM disciplines under the microscope. In this chapter, Joan Ferrini-Mundy and Beste Güçler examine specific institutional initiatives to improve undergraduate STEM education. Each STEM field has a distinctive culture, vocabulary, and modes of operation. The authors examine strategies to enhance the climate for STEM education within the unique contexts of different disciplines and identify common practices that many STEM fields are using to enhance undergraduate STEM

NEW DIRECTIONS FOR TEACHING AND LEARNING • DOI: 10.1002/tl

education. The examples they present provide instructive models that can promote creative thought, experimentation, and improved educational practice in other STEM fields.

Creating a supportive climate for teaching and learning in STEM is more than an institutional or even a higher education concern. Chapter Six provides a national perspective on the issue of STEM undergraduate education. Judith A. Ramaley explains why improvements to STEM education are a national priority and discusses how national-level organizations such as the National Science Foundation and others can help to shape a STEM culture that values and rewards efforts to strengthen education in STEM fields.

Efforts to enhance undergraduate education in STEM fields must reach out to and engage future faculty, or the impact of these initiatives will be limited and short term. In Chapter Seven, Ann E. Austin and colleagues examine how doctoral education in STEM fields socializes future faculty. They conclude that many STEM doctoral programs do not provide adequate opportunities for graduate students to learn about and prepare for teaching roles in research universities or other types of postsecondary institutions. The chapter also reviews important national and institutional programs designed to prepare future faculty more systematically for their roles as educators. One prime example is the Preparing Future Faculty Program, which promotes faculty preparation across a wide range of disciplines. Another example is the Center for the Integration of Research, Teaching, and Learning (CIRTL), which focuses specifically on the preparation of educators in STEM fields. The chapter gives an overview of the objectives and methods of these national efforts to prepare future faculty. It also provides detailed profiles of programs to prepare aspiring STEM educators at two CIRTL-affiliated institutions (University of Wisconsin–Madison and Michigan State University). The models presented in Chapter Seven provide a constructive starting point for individual institutions or teams of institutions wishing to do a better job of preparing their graduate students for roles as STEM educators.

The final chapter highlights key ideas and recommendations that earlier chapter authors advance. It acknowledges that improving the climate for undergraduate education in STEM fields is a complex challenge requiring coordinated systemic action. This chapter considers actions that STEM stakeholders must take to create a climate conducive to strengthening the quality and effectiveness of STEM education in colleges and universities.

Roger G. Baldwin
Editor

ROGER G. BALDWIN is professor of educational administration and coordinator of the Higher, Adult, and Lifelong Education Graduate Program at Michigan State University.

Acknowledgements

The editor wishes to express his appreciation to Deborah Chang and Jean Beland of Michigan State University for invaluable research and editing assistance. Their support and persistence helped to translate this volume from an interesting idea to a completed document.

1

Many stakeholders must cooperate to improve STEM undergraduate education.

The Climate for Undergraduate Teaching and Learning in STEM Fields

Roger G. Baldwin

Undergraduate education in the STEM fields (science, technology, engineering, and mathematics) needs improvement, a conclusion that multiple national reports over the past two decades have reached (American Association of Physics Teachers, 1996; National Research Council, 1989; National Science Foundation, 1996; Steen, 1987). In 2007, Brainard argued that efforts to enhance teaching in STEM fields continue to encounter resistance. Critiques of STEM education may emphasize different aspects of the STEM undergraduate education problem. Nevertheless, each delivers one clear and consistent message: undergraduate education in STEM fields is not adequate to the task of preparing workers for our technologically driven economy or developing a scientifically literate citizenry capable of engaging in informed dialogue and decision making on important public policy issues.

The report of the National Research Council's Committee on Undergraduate Science Education (1999) describes a nation divided into a technologically knowledgeable elite and a disadvantaged majority (National Research Council, 1999). The challenge facing educators in STEM is great. They need to "teach large numbers of students with diverse backgrounds and interests" (National Research Council, 2003, p. 2) and prepare them for a rapidly changing world where science and technology are increasingly important. As Nobel laureate Carl Wieman (2007) observed, "We need a more scientifically literate populace to address the global challenges that humanity now faces and that only science can explain and possibly mitigate, such as global warming, as well as to make wise decisions, informed

NEW DIRECTIONS FOR TEACHING AND LEARNING, no. 117, Spring 2009 © Wiley Periodicals, Inc.
Published online in Wiley InterScience (www.interscience.wiley.com) • DOI: 10.1002/tl.340

9

by scientific understanding, about issues such as genetic modification" (p. 9). To fulfill these objectives adequately, STEM teaching practices need to be more inclusive and flexible as the United States becomes increasingly diverse. If STEM education maintains a business-as-usual stance, our society will lose talent that we need in a competitive global economy (National Science Foundation, 1996) and an increasingly interdependent world.

Status of Teaching in STEM Fields

Many institutions are working to enhance teaching and learning in their STEM classrooms and laboratories, and many individual STEM faculty members and instructional teams are working hard to improve their instructional strategies. Harvard's Eric Mazur and the University of British Columbia's Carl Wieman are prominent examples. Each has implemented widely acclaimed innovative instructional strategies in undergraduate physics education (Brainard, 2007). At the same time, reports on the overall status of teaching in STEM fields are a source for concern. They tell us that a large proportion of STEM faculty have received little formal training in effective teaching techniques or how to assess learning. Generally STEM instructors teach as they were taught. Their approach to instruction is rarely influenced by learning theory or recent research on cognitive science (National Research Council, 2003).

Detailed studies of STEM teaching practices (Seymour and Hewitt, 1997) paint a fuller picture of the underlying problem with STEM undergraduate education. Many undergraduate classes occur in large lecture halls where instructional practices are constrained by architecture and seating arrangements. In addition, students complain about the poor quality of STEM teaching, especially in large lower-level classes, where student-teacher dialogue is limited. Undergraduate education in many STEM classes is heavily lecture based, encouraging students to be passive learners (National Research Council, 2003). In this environment, many students rely heavily on memorization of facts and formulas to pass tests (Brainard, 2007) and may fail to achieve genuine understanding of the STEM subject matter. Research shows that students retain only a fraction of the information presented in the typical lecture. Moreover, the traditional lecture is not an effective way to help students master the basic scientific concepts essential to advanced study and work in STEM fields (Wieman, 2007).

Specific criticisms Seymour and Hewitt report include instructors' limited use of illustrations to clarify their points and achieve understanding of scientific concepts and processes. Similarly, they note the sparse discussion in many STEM classes of the practical applications and implications of the subject matter covered. Derek Bok, in *Our Underachieving Colleges* (2006), explains that teaching in basic mathematics courses is "likely to emphasize memorizing abstract rules, employed in formal, abstract ways, with little opportunity to consider applications to real life" (p. 130). Reports on the nature of STEM teaching also describe the ineffective use of instructional technology in classes and mechanical lab exercises that fail to emulate the challenging and engaging process of scientific discovery. Bok also criticizes "cookbook problem solving" (p. 261) in undergraduate STEM courses.

Equally troubling is the climate that pervades many STEM classrooms and educational programs. Many introductory STEM classes have a competitive atmosphere that assumes a lot of students are not capable of succeeding. Bok's comprehensive analysis of undergraduate education highlighted one likely source of this problem. Many introductory science courses are designed to build a foundation for students who intend to major in the field and possibly obtain a doctorate. Often these courses cover vast quantities of information that is considered essential for advanced study but is not necessary for a basic understanding of the field (Bok, 2006). Such courses can act as a filter, weeding out less desirable students whose interest in the subject matter is less certain or less intense. The atmosphere in such classes can signal many potential students that they do not fit in STEM fields or are not welcome. Hence, many students who could benefit from studying science and mathematics choose to transfer into other academic fields (National Research Council, 2003; National Science Foundation, 1996).

Forces Promoting Change in STEM Undergraduate Education

In spite of ongoing problems, there is good reason to be optimistic about the long-term future of undergraduate education in STEM fields. Many forces are advancing the cause of change and reform. Research in cognitive science and education has advanced understanding of the teaching and learning process (National Research Council, 2003). Brainard (2007) concluded from his investigation of the state of science teaching that new teaching models "have shown success in engaging and retaining undergraduates" (p. 16). A good example is North Carolina State's Scale-Up teaching method, which provides a highly collaborative, hands-on, computer-rich, interactive learning environment for large-enrollment courses (Physics Education Research Group, 2007). Scale-Up reduced the failure rate to one-third of what is normal and dramatically reduced the failure rate of women and students from underrepresented groups (Brainard, 2007; Physics Education Research Group, 2007).

There is a great demand for scientifically trained workers to fuel our technologically driven economy. This need is compounded due to increasing global competition. Changes in the U.S. economy make clear that workers with strong backgrounds in science and technology fare much better in the workforce than do workers who lack scientific knowledge and skills.

Our ever more diverse population demands scientific education that is welcoming and accessible to many types of learners. Awareness is growing of the need to include diverse types of students in STEM fields if our society is to have the skilled labor force it needs to enhance our standard of living and remain competitive in a global marketplace.

A large cadre of educational leaders and leading professional associations strongly advocates improvements in STEM education at the undergraduate level. Many influential groups and organizations acknowledge the need to reform STEM education and are working to improve undergraduate teaching and learning in STEM fields. A host of articles, reports, and books have appeared in recent years critiquing current practice and advocating improvements in STEM undergraduate educational strategies. Many professional organizations and disciplinary societies have joined the reform chorus, imploring their members and stakeholders to adopt more flexible, active, collaborative, and welcoming pedagogical practices that will reach out more effectively to diverse learners. The American Chemical Society is one example of an organization that promotes dialogue and action to improve undergraduate education in scientific fields. It publishes a journal on chemical education, provides instructional resources, and sponsors a variety of workshops on strategies to enhance chemistry instruction and student learning. Likewise, some accrediting organizations, such as ABET (Accreditation Board for Engineering and Technology), the chief accreditor of engineering education programs, are now heavily involved in efforts to strengthen undergraduate education in their specific fields.

Together these powerful developments and influential organizations comprise a potent force for change in the standard ways that STEM undergraduate education is delivered. Their combined efforts have promoted a national dialogue on the STEM education challenge as well as many institutional and individual faculty efforts to improve undergraduate education in STEM fields. It would seem that the synergy created by these many complementary efforts to improve undergraduate STEM education would be irresistible. However, reform has been slow and erratic, taking root in some places but not others. Often creative new initiatives have lost momentum over time as forces of inertia (which every scientist knows are both natural and inevitable) take hold.

Barriers to Reform in STEM Undergraduate Education

Many factors account for the slow, sporadic pace of reform in undergraduate STEM education. Certainly the limited training of STEM faculty for their teaching roles is a factor. The lack of knowledge of the teaching and learning literature and the many types of instructional strategies places limits on what many STEM faculty do in their classrooms and laboratories to encourage undergraduate learning.

The faculty evaluation and reward system in place in many higher education institutions also discourages efforts to enhance undergraduate education in STEM fields. With the faculty reward system balanced in most STEM fields on the side of research (National Science Foundation, 1996), many faculty members choose to invest their limited discretionary time in their research and writing for publication rather than their teaching.

Overall, the climate in many colleges and universities and in the academic profession as a whole does not seem conducive to enhancing undergraduate education in STEM. Many reports discuss the lack of resources to support pedagogical development in STEM (National Science Foundation, 1996) and the absence of incentives to study the literature on teaching and learning (National Research Council, 2003). Similarly, the limited rewards for course and instructional improvements discourage STEM professors from investing the time and energy required to update and upgrade their approaches to instruction (National Science Foundation, 1996). The National Research Council, National Science Foundation, American Chemical Society, and other organizations advocate reform in STEM education and publish materials on how to implement educational improvements. At the same time, this information on good instructional practice has not had a widespread impact on STEM education at the undergraduate level. The autonomy of discipline-based departments and the freedom of faculty members to run their classrooms as they wish certainly inhibit widespread change.

Today many of the efforts to strengthen undergraduate education in STEM continue to rely on individual faculty or small faculty groups who are committed to the cause of improving science or technology education in their department or institution. Daniel Udovic's Workshop Biology at the University of Oregon, which replaced traditional science lectures with a series of active, inquiry-based modules, is a good example of one's professor's effort to improve teaching and learning in his discipline. Another is Janine Trempy's course, The World According to Microbes, at Oregon State University. This problem-based, cross-disciplinary course integrates science, mathematics, and engineering and serves both majors and nonmajors (Handelsman and others, 2004). Trempy equated her own experience as an undergraduate student in general science courses to "long-winded lectures, intimidating tests and non-applicable lab experiments" (Oregon State University News and Communication Services, 1996). A citation naming her the 1996 Oregon Professor of the Year explains Trempy's determination "to create courses where students acted, rather than just listened. Where they worked together to solve real problems. Where they remembered what they learned. And where students ranging from philosophy to physical education worked together to share their expertise and learn directly from each other" (Oregon State University News and Communication Services, 1996). Regrettably, individual science teaching innovations like these have been slow to catch on. "Reform has been initiated by a few pioneers, while many other scientists have actively resisted changing their teaching (Handelsman and others, 2004).

Fortunately, the innovative teaching strategies of some STEM professors have gained considerable attention and influenced the instructional practices of colleagues far beyond their own campuses. Carl Wieman's experiments with personal-response systems ("clickers") and Eric Mazur's peer instruction technique are noteworthy examples (Wieman, 2007). However, it is doubtful that profound change in STEM undergraduate education can be achieved through the bold and creative initiatives of single professors working hard to enhance the learning of students in their STEM classes. The history of STEM undergraduate education shows that reform at the level of the individual professor is not sufficient to implement the holistic change needed to transform STEM undergraduate education. This fact does not minimize the important role individual professors and faculty groups must play in creating a climate for enhancing teaching and learning in STEM fields. However, as Susan Millar, a senior scientist in the School of Education at the University of Wisconsin–Madison, has observed, "I don't know that you can take these kinds of [innovative STEM education] programs to scale when the unit of change is the individual" (Brainard, 2007, p. A17).

Improving the Climate for Strengthening Undergraduate Education in STEM

Many elements of the formula for implementing comprehensive reform of STEM undergraduate education are in place. Yet the climate for enhancing STEM undergraduate education remains challenging, if not hostile. No single action or initiative, no matter how substantial or well meaning, seems adequate to catalyze widespread reform of STEM undergraduate education that reaches the level of specific STEM departments and individual classrooms and laboratories. Many actions, inside and outside higher education, are needed to improve the environment for enhancing teaching and learning in STEM.

The lone wolf approach to improving STEM undergraduate education is not sufficient to meet the challenge of preparing a technologically competent workforce and a scientifically literate citizenry. Many STEM education innovations and improvements will not survive, let alone proliferate, without major changes in the STEM culture and the policies and practices of higher education.

This analysis of the current climate surrounding STEM undergraduate education suggests that a number of complementary initiatives are necessary to make that climate more conducive to widespread and lasting reform. First, STEM faculty need ready access to practical, easy-to-apply information on how students learn. They also need opportunities to learn about effective instructional strategies. Dialogue with colleagues on teaching challenges and opportunities to experiment with varied instructional techniques is one way to foster a climate receptive to STEM educational reform. Revisions of evaluation and reward policies, including the criteria for tenure and promotion, are another step necessary to improve the climate for strengthening undergraduate STEM education. Until investments in improving teaching yield consequential recognition and rewards, faculty will favor research when they set priorities and distribute their limited time. Rewarding scholarship on teaching and learning in STEM fields is another way to enhance the climate for strengthening undergraduate teaching and learning. Giving meaningful professional credit to STEM educators for studying the learning process in their classes and labs will reinforce their efforts to improve their teaching. Incentives for experimentation and innovation in the classroom are also needed to improve the climate for undergraduate education in STEM. Moving beyond conventional instructional methods in STEM requires professors to try out new and unfamiliar techniques that may or may not work with their students. The culture of science values a spirit of risk taking and innovation in the laboratory or the field. It should also promote experimentation in the classroom by rewarding faculty for their efforts and not penalizing them when well-intended educational innovations do not live up to their original promise.

Creating a climate for improving undergraduate STEM education requires a collaborative effort at many levels. Scientific organizations and professional societies are an important part of the equation for success. They should examine the effectiveness of their efforts to communicate with STEM educators and ask how they can be more helpful in promoting change. In particular, influential organizations such as the National Science Foundation, National Resource Council, STEM accrediting agencies, and others have an important role to play as agents of cultural change. They can use their considerable resources and influence to stress the importance of enhanced undergraduate education to the future vitality of STEM fields.

Institutional leaders, including presidents, provosts, and deans, also have a critical role to play in creating a climate that supports improvements in STEM undergraduate education. They can focus attention on the STEM education issue and allocate resources to support key reform initiatives. By publicly identifying STEM education as a priority, they can promote useful dialogue and action. Without the stimulus that key institutional leaders can provide, the status quo in STEM education is likely to prevail on most campuses.

Genuine reform of STEM undergraduate education must take root at the department level, or all other efforts to promote improvement will be meaningless. Individual departments, led by their chair and respected colleagues, must engage the STEM education issue within their own environment. They should look for barriers to educational improvements and identify concrete actions they can take to strengthen the undergraduate education they provide. If sustainable reform is to occur, departments must consider how they can use their teaching assignments, faculty and budgetary resources, evaluation criteria, and rewards to promote innovation and improvements in their undergraduate programs.

Professors who experiment with educational improvements in their classrooms and share their experiences and outcomes with colleagues help to develop a culture of improvement in their departments and institutions.

Similarly, STEM faculty members who meet regularly to talk about teaching and learning issues or to discuss books or reports on effective teaching practices also help to build a climate that supports improvements in STEM undergraduate education.

Conclusion

A meteorologist looking at the climate for undergraduate teaching and learning in STEM fields might conclude that the forecast is mixed. There are positive signs on the horizon as well as some threatening conditions. This forecaster might conclude there is a 50 percent chance that the climate for STEM education will improve substantially.

When the weather forecast is less than favorable, all we can do is complain or take a defensive stance and seek shelter. Fortunately, the climate for improving undergraduate STEM education can be improved substantially by the actions of many concerned stakeholders: professors, educational leaders, professional societies, and government agencies, among others. We hope that each will choose to play a role in this important effort to strengthen undergraduate education in STEM fields.

References

American Association of Physics Teachers. *Physics at the Crossroads: Innovation and Revitalization in Undergraduate Physics-Plans for Action. Executive Summary.* Proceedings of the American Association of Physics Teachers Physics at the Crossroads Conference. College Park, Md.: American Association of Physics Teachers, 1996.

Bok, D. *Our Underachieving Colleges: A Candid Look at How Much Students Learn and Why They Should Be Learning More.* Princeton, N.J.: Princeton University Press, 2006.

Brainard, J. "The Tough Road to Better Science Teaching." *Chronicle of Higher Education,* Aug. 3, 2007, pp. 16–18.

Handelsman, J., and others. "Scientific Teaching." *Science,* 2004, *304,* 521–522.

National Research Council. *Everybody Counts: A Report to the Nation on the Future of Mathematics Education.* Washington, D.C.: National Research Council and Mathematical Sciences Education Board (MSEB), 1989.

National Research Council. *Transforming Undergraduate Education in Science, Mathematics, Engineering, and Technology.* Washington, D.C.: National Academy Press, 1999.

National Research Council. *Evaluating and Improving Undergraduate Teaching in Science, Technology, Engineering and Mathematics.* Washington, D.C.: National Academies Press, 2003.

National Science Foundation. *Shaping the Future: New Expectations for Undergraduate Education in Science, Mathematics, Engineering, and Technology.* Arlington, Va.: National Science Foundation, 1996.

Physics Education Research Group. "About the SCALE-UP Project." 2007. Retrieved Aug. 30, 2007, from http://www.ncsu.edu/PER/scaleup.html.

Seymour, E., and Hewitt, N. M. *Talking About Leaving: Why Undergraduates Leave the Sciences.* Boulder, Colo.: Westview Press, 1997.

Stauth, D. "Top Oregon Prof: Participatory Science Key to Learning." 1996. Retrieved Sept. 19, 2007, from http://oregonstate.edu/dept/nce/newsarch/1996/96October/profyear.htm.

Steen, L. A. (ed.). *Calculus for a New Century: A Pump, Not a Filter*. Washington, D.C.: Mathematical Association of America, 1987.

Wieman, C. "Why Not Try: A Scientific Approach to Science Education?" *Change*, 2007, *39*(5), 9–15.

ROGER G. BALDWIN *is professor of educational administration and coordinator of the Higher, Adult, and Lifelong Education Graduate Program at Michigan State University.*

NEW DIRECTIONS FOR TEACHING AND LEARNING • DOI: 10.1002/tl

2

This chapter provides faculty with design principles based on the How People Learn framework, as well as current best practices for designing engaged learning environments in STEM classes in the hope of continuing improvement in STEM education.

Supportive Teaching and Learning Strategies in STEM Education

Karl A. Smith, Tameka Clarke Douglas, Monica F. Cox

The 1996 Advisory Committee report to the National Science Foundation, *Shaping the Future: New Expectations for Undergraduate Education in Science, Mathematics, Engineering, and Technology,* called for many changes in STEM (science, technology, engineering, and mathematics) education (George and others, 1996). The committee's overriding recommendation was that "all students have access to supportive, excellent undergraduate education in science, mathematics, engineering, and technology, and all students learn these subjects by direct experience with the methods and processes of inquiry" (p. ii). One of their recommendations for faculty was highly salient for this chapter:

> Believe and affirm that every student can learn, and model good practices that increase learning; starting with the student's experience, but have high expectations within a supportive climate; and build inquiry, a sense of wonder and the excitement of discovery, plus communication and teamwork, critical thinking, and life-long learning skills into learning experiences [p. iv].

Seymour and Hewitt's three-year ethnographic study (1997) of 335 science, mathematics, and engineering (SME) students across seven institutions indicated that there were no identifiable academic differences between students that were significant enough to explain why one group chose to leave SME disciplines while the others remain. However, both groups, regardless of race and gender, voiced greatest concern for the "chilly

New Directions for Teaching and Learning, no. 117, Spring 2009 © Wiley Periodicals, Inc.
Published online in Wiley InterScience (www.interscience.wiley.com) • DOI: 10.1002/tl.341

climate" and poor-quality learning environments. High rates of student attrition were more reliant on students' perception of the quality and character of education in SME and less on students' academic abilities.

Tinto's interactionalist theory of college student departure (1993) also identifies the climate as a major reason that students leave college. In exploring theories of academic and social integration, Tinto states that the extent to which students persist at an institution relates to their educational and institutional commitments. Factors that also come into play include students' background characteristics and the extent to which students are socially and academically integrated into the university culture. Students who are socially integrated are more likely to persist at an institution, demonstrating institutional commitment, and if they are academically integrated, students are more likely to graduate within their chosen majors, demonstrating educational commitment. The normative dimension of academic integration relates to students' interpretations of the academic climate at an institution and is present when students' intellectual development and the intellectual climate of an institution are aligned (Tinto, 1975; Braxton, 2000). Clearly the classroom lies at the heart of students' academic experiences.

As Nobel laureate Herbert Simon (1996) stated, "The meaning of 'knowing' has shifted from being able to remember and repeat information to being able to find and use it" (p. 1). The NSF *Shaping the Future* report (George and others, 1996) recommends a shift in the paradigm of STEM education to creating a climate of engagement and exciting all students to explore and discover the knowledge within science, technology, engineering, and mathematics.

Over ten years have passed since the *Shaping the Future* report and Seymour and Hewitt's *Talking About Leaving*. Current reports such as *Rising Above the Gathering Storm* (Augustine, 2005) indicate growing concern about STEM teaching and learning. Can the state of the learning environment in STEM classrooms change substantially? What can faculty do to design more supportive learning environments that include all students?

We think the answer to the first question is yes and provide a summary of the state of the art of thinking about the design of supportive learning environments. The key ideas are designing learning environments based on the How People Learn framework and working backward from student learning outcomes, through evidence, to planning instruction.

Recent reports, however, conclude that higher education in general, and presumably STEM education, is "declining by degrees" (Hersh and Merrow, 2005) and is "underachieving" (Bok, 2005). While the conclusion seems to be that postsecondary education is not performing well, there is a lack of focus on how to improve it. Sullivan (2005), in his overview of professionalism in America, highlights the problems associated with competition (negative interdependence) and advocates the cooperation inherent in "civic professionalism." He proposes that professional education may be renewed through three apprenticeships: an apprenticeship of the head that focuses on intellectual or cognitive development, an apprenticeship of the hand that focuses on the tacit knowledge and skills practiced by competent practitioners, and an apprenticeship of the heart that focuses on the attitudes and values shared by the professional community. Thus, it is not only more academic focus that is needed, but also practical skills and civic values. An instructional procedure that affects the head and hand while simultaneously affecting the heart, thereby potentially reversing the negative trends noted in higher education, is cooperative learning (Smith, Sheppard, Johnson, and Johnson, 2005; Johnson, Johnson, and Smith, 2007).

The How People Learn Framework and the Backward Design Approach

Before elaborating on cooperative learning, problem-based learning, and other forms of pedagogies of engagement, which we argue will provide substantially better learning environments, we summarize the How People Learn framework and the backward design approach because these provide compelling reasons, as well as the necessary conditions, to embrace pedagogies of engagement.

How People Learn Framework. Although the individual lenses (see Figure 2.1) represent aspects of a classroom, interdependencies of these lenses have been found to be more common within classroom environments

Figure 2.1. Four Lenses That Make Up the How People Learn Framework.

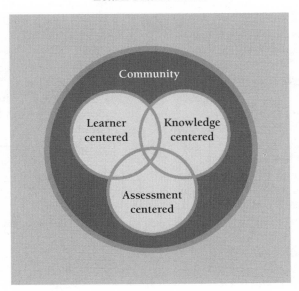

Source: Adapted from Bransford, Vye, and Bateman (2002).

(Cox, 2005). Each lens has criteria for careful consideration in the light of the subject matter, course level, and desired outcome. Lenses are complementary, and all lenses should be present and in balance to create an effective learning environment (Bransford, Brown, and Cocking, 2000; Bransford, Vye, and Bateman, 2002). A learning environment that is *knowledge centered* is designed based on an analysis of what we want students to know and be able to do as a result of the learning experience and helps students develop the foundational and enduring knowledge, skills, and attitudes needed for successful transfer of this knowledge. A learner-centered environment connects the strengths, interests, and preconceptions of learners to their current academic tasks and learning goals and helps students learn about themselves as learners. *Community centered* means providing a supportive, enriched, and flexible setting inside and outside the classroom where all students can learn, feel safe to ask questions, and work collaboratively. Finally, *assessment centered* means providing multiple opportunities to monitor and make visible students' progress from what they currently understand to the ultimate learning goals in an effort to allow students to continue working on their weaknesses and revise their thinking.

Our principal How People Learn guide for this chapter is "Creating High-Quality Learning Environments: Guidelines from Research on How People Learn" (Bransford, Vye, and Bateman, 2002). We chose this as our guide for three reasons: it was part of a National Academy of Sciences workshop, it is focused on postsecondary education, and it connects the How People Learn framework to the backward design approach of Wiggins and McTighe in *Understanding by Design* (1998).

We also note that another recent *New Directions for Teaching and Learning* volume (Number 108) applied the How People Learn framework (Petrosino, Martin, and Svihla, 2006). Petrosino, Martin, and Svihla (2006) focused more on adaptive expertise and the STAR (Software Technology for Action and Reflection) legacy cycle, and hence our chapter is complementary to their volume. Bransford (2007) stressed the importance of thoughtfully designed learning environments in his recent guest editorial in the *Journal of Engineering Education,* and Pellegrino (2006) argues for rethinking and redesigning curriculum in his paper commissioned by the National Center on Education and the Economy for the New Commission on the Skills of the American Workforce.

Backward Design Process. The idea of a backward-looking design process from student learning outcomes, through acceptable evidence, especially feedback and assessment, to planning instruction has been and is being embraced by others; Dee Fink, for example, has significant learning experiences in which he adds emphasis on situational factors that influence the design (Fink, 2003).

Identifying Desired Outcomes. The first step in the backward design model is identifying what it is you want students to know, to be able to do, and perhaps even to be as a result of the class session, learning module, course, or program. In STEM classes, learning outcomes are typically framed as cognitive outcomes: what we want the students to know. Two additional dimensions of outcome are what we want students to be able to do and who we want the students to be, that is, the values and attitudes shared by members of the community as a result of the designed learning experience. Sullivan (2005) frames these three outcome areas as the three apprenticeships.

Wiggins and McTighe (1997) recommend identifying (1) big ideas, topics, or processes that have enduring value beyond the classroom; (2) ideas, topics, or processes that reside at the heart of the discipline; and (3) ideas, topics, or processes that require uncoverage, that is, complex and difficult-to-learn ideas that require faculty guidance and insights. Finally, in planning for pedagogies of engagement, Wiggins and McTighe recommend considering to what extent the idea, topic, or process offers potential for engaging students.

Assessment. The second step in the model is determining acceptable evidence to decide whether or to what extent students have met the learning goals. Typically this is done with content-focused questions measuring outcomes at the low end of Bloom's taxonomy: Remember, Understand (Anderson and Krathwohl, 2001). To assess student learning outcomes at the mid and upper levels of Bloom's Taxonomy—Apply, Analyze, Evaluate, Create—open-ended questions and problems are typically used. Recently there has been considerable interest in using tasks that approximate practice and are more authentic and performance based.

Assessing students in groups creates additional opportunities and challenges for assessing student learning. Our recommendation for faculty who use cooperative learning groups is to design, encourage, and support students' learning in groups but assess individual learning and performance (Smith, 1998; Johnson and Johnson, 2004).

In addition to the summative assessment of student learning, it is also important to provide formative and diagnostic assessment opportunities for students (Angelo and Cross, 1993). More than summative assessments, formative assessments help teachers revise their teaching practices, identify and mitigate potential problems and hindrances to student learning, and note changes in student learning throughout a course. Related to students, formative assessments help students self-assess their understandings of academic content, support a student-centered approach to learning, and provide an additional method to document this learning (Angelo and Cross, 1993; Bransford, Vye, and Bateman, 2002). Technology such as wireless classroom communication systems also have been used extensively within both K–12 and postsecondary settings to increase the amount of formative assessment that occurs within classroom environments (Pea and Gomez, 1992; Dufresne and others, 1996; Mestre, Gerace, Dufresne, and Leonard, 1997; Wenk and others, 1997; Roselli and Brophy, 2002).

In the absence of technology, instructors may use other classroom assessment techniques to assess students formatively (Angelo and Cross, 1993). For example, the minute paper technique asks students to give a two- to three-minute response on index cards about what they are learning in the class and what questions remain unanswered. Similar to the minute paper, the "muddiest point" gives an instructor quick feedback about students' understanding. Within this technique, students are asked to identify the most confusing or most difficult aspect of a lesson. Additional techniques may be used by instructors depending on the information that they want to obtain from their students.

Plan Instruction. The third step in the backward design process is planning instruction. We focus on pedagogies of engagement—cooperative learning and problem-based learning—for learning outcomes that represent big ideas, are at the heart of the discipline, require uncoverage, and have potential for engaging students.

Implementation of Cooperative Learning and Problem-Based Learning

The classroom practices involved with cooperative learning and problem-based learning are complex to design, implement, and manage. In part because of these implementation challenges and many others, cooperative learning and problem-based learning are not widely practiced in STEM classrooms. Part of the reason for this may be not only their difficulty in designing, implementing, and managing, but that most faculty did not experience any form of cooperative or problem-based learning during their undergraduate or graduate education.

In this section, we highlight some well-developed and well-honed practices. Informal cooperative learning groups (often referred to as active learning), formal cooperative learning groups, and cooperative base groups are the most commonly implemented by engineering faculty. Each has a place in providing opportunities for students to be intellectually active and personally interactive in and outside the classroom. Informal cooperative learning is commonly used in predominantly lecture classes and will be described only briefly. Formal cooperative learning can be used in content-intensive classes where the mastery of conceptual or procedural material is essential; however, many faculty find it easier to start in recitation or laboratory sections or design project courses. Base groups are long-term cooperative learning groups whose principal responsibility is to provide support and encouragement for all members, that is, to ensure that each member gets the help he or she needs to be successful in the course and in college.

Active Learning. Informal cooperative learning consists of having students work together to achieve a joint learning goal in temporary, ad hoc groups that last from a few minutes to one class period (Johnson, Johnson, and Smith, 1998). Informal cooperative learning groups also ensure that misconceptions, incorrect understanding, and gaps in understanding are identified and corrected and learning experiences are personalized. In one instantiation of informal cooperative learning, every ten to fifteen minutes,

Figure 2.2. Bookends on a Class Session

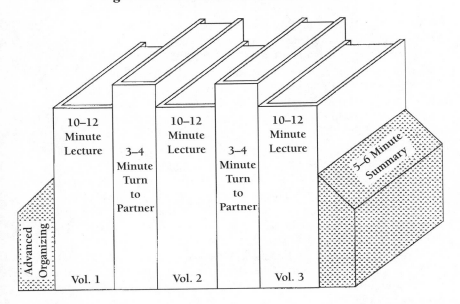

students are asked to discuss and process what they are learning as shown in the bookends on a class session (Figure 2.2).

Breaking up lectures with short cooperative processing times results in slightly less lecture time but reengages the students. During lecturing and direct teaching, the instructor ensures that students do the intellectual work of organizing material, explaining it, summarizing it, and integrating it into existing conceptual networks. Common informal cooperative learning techniques include focused discussions before and after the lecture (bookends) and interspersing turn-to-your-partner discussions throughout the lecture. Although three- to four-minute turn-to-your-partner discussions are illustrated in Figure 2.2, many faculty provide one to two minutes, and some can be as short as thirty seconds.

As faculty gain familiarity with real-time assessment and informal cooperative learning, they often modify the format. For example, if most students choose the correct answer to a concept question, the faculty member might ask students to reflect on the underlying rationale for their answer and turn to their neighbor to discuss it; if most students choose an incorrect answer to a concept question, the faculty member might try to explain it again, perhaps in a different way; and if the answers to the concept question are a mixture of correct and incorrect, the faculty member might ask students to turn to their neighbor, compare answers, and see if they can reach agreement on an answer.

Many examples of the use of informal cooperative learning are available. Mazur (1997) describes the interactive aspects of a nineteen-minute lecture on Newton's laws in his book *Peer Instruction*. Darmofal (2005) has written about his use of informal cooperative learning and concept tests in aeronautical engineering, and Martin, Mitchell, and Newell (2003) have been experimenting with informal cooperative learning and concept tests in fluid mechanics.

Informal cooperative learning ensures that students are actively involved in understanding what they are learning. It also provides time for instructors to gather their wits, reorganize notes, take a deep breath, and move around the class listening to what students are saying. Listening to student discussions can give instructors direction and insight into how well students understand the concepts and material being taught.

The importance of faculty engaging students in introductory courses, using procedures such as those summarized, is stressed by Seymour's research (2002): "The greatest single challenge to SMET pedagogical reform remains the problem of whether and how large classes can be infused with more active and interactive learning methods" (p. 87).

Formal Cooperative Learning Groups. Formal cooperative learning groups are more structured than informal cooperative learning groups, are given more complex tasks, and typically stay together longer. Social interdependence theory and cooperative learning research identified five essential elements to successful implementation of formal cooperative learning groups: positive interdependence, face-to-face promotive interaction, individual accountability and personal responsibility, teamwork skills, and group processing:

- *Positive interdependence.* The heart of cooperative learning is positive interdependence. Students must believe that they are linked with others in a way that one cannot succeed unless the other members of the group succeed (and vice versa). Students are working together to get the job done. In other words, they must perceive that they sink or swim together. In formal cooperative learning groups, positive interdependence may be structured by asking group members to agree on an answer for the group (group product—goal interdependence), making sure each member can explain the group's answer (learning goal interdependence), and fulfilling assigned role responsibilities (role interdependence). Other ways of structuring positive interdependence include having common rewards such as a shared grade (reward interdependence), shared resources (resource interdependence), or a division of labor (task interdependence).
- *Face-to-face promotive interaction.* Once a professor establishes positive interdependence, he or she must ensure that students interact to help each other accomplish the task and promote each other's success. Students are expected to explain orally to each other how to solve problems, discuss with each other the nature of the concepts and strategies being learned, teach their knowledge to classmates, explain to each other the

connections between present and past learning, and help, encourage, and support each other's efforts to learn. Silent students are uninvolved students who are certainly not contributing to the learning of others and may not be contributing to their own learning.

- *Individual accountability and personal responsibility.* One purpose of cooperative learning groups is to make each member a stronger individual in his or her own right. Students learn together so that they can subsequently perform better as individuals. To ensure that each member is strengthened, students are held individually accountable to do their share of the work. The performance of each student is assessed and the results given back to the individual and perhaps to the group. The group needs to know who needs more assistance in completing the assignment, and group members need to know they cannot "hitchhike" on the work of others. Common ways to structure individual accountability include giving individual exams, self and peer assessment, and randomly calling on individual students to report on their group's efforts.
- *Teamwork skills.* Contributing to the success of a cooperative effort requires teamwork skills, including skills in leadership, decision making, trust building, communication, and conflict management. These skills have to be taught just as purposefully and precisely as academic skills. Many students have never worked cooperatively in learning situations and therefore lack the needed teamwork skills for doing so effectively. Faculty often introduce and emphasize teamwork skills through assigning differentiated roles to each group member. For example, students learn about documenting group work by serving as the task recorder, developing strategy and monitoring how the group is working by serving as process recorder, providing direction to the group by serving as coordinator, and ensuring that everyone in the group understands and can explain by serving as the checker. Teamwork skills are being emphasized by employers and the ABET Engineering Criteria 2000, and several books and articles are available to help students develop teamwork skills (Johnson and Johnson, 2000; Shuman, Besterfield-Sacre, and McGourty, 2005; Smith and Imbrie, 2007).
- *Group processing.* Professors need to ensure that members of each cooperative learning group discuss how well they are achieving their goals and maintaining effective working relationships. Groups need to describe what member actions are helpful and unhelpful and make decisions about what to continue or change. Such processing enables learning groups to focus on group maintenance, facilitates the learning of collaborative skills, ensures that members receive feedback on their participation, and reminds students to practice collaborative skills consistently. Some of the keys to successful processing are allowing sufficient time for it to take place, making it specific rather than vague, maintaining student involvement in processing, reminding students to use their teamwork skills during processing, and ensuring that clear expectations as to the purpose of processing have been communicated. A common procedure

for group processing is to ask each group to list at least three things the group did well and at least one thing that could be improved.

These five essential elements of a well-structured formal cooperative learning group are nearly identical to those of high-performance teams in business and industry as identified by Katzenbach and Smith (1993): "A team is a *small number* of people with *complementary skills* who are committed to a *common purpose, performance goals,* and *approach* for which they hold themselves *mutually accountable*" (p. 45).

Many faculty who believe that they are using cooperative learning are missing its essence. There is a crucial difference between simply putting students in groups to learn and in structuring cooperation among students. Cooperation is *not* having students sit side-by-side at the same table to talk with each other as they do their individual assignments. Cooperation is *not* assigning a report to a group of students where one student does all the work and the others put their names on the product as well. Cooperation is *not* having students do a task individually with instructions that the ones who finish first are to help the slower students. Cooperation is much more than being physically near other students, discussing material with other students, helping other students, or sharing material among students, although each of these is important in cooperative learning.

Before choosing and implementing a formal cooperative learning strategy, there are several conditions that should be evaluated to determine whether it is the best approach for the situation: there should be sufficient time available for students to work in groups both inside and outside the classroom; the task should be complex enough to warrant a formal group; and the instructor's goals should include the development of skills of the types that have been shown to be affected positively by cooperative learning, such as critical thinking, higher-level reasoning, and teamwork skills.

The detailed aspects of the instructor's role in structuring formal cooperative learning groups are described in Johnson, Johnson, and Smith (1998): (1) specify the objectives for the lesson, (2) make a number of instructional decisions (for example, group size and determining a method of assigning students to groups), (3) explain the task and the positive interdependence, (4) monitor students' learning and intervene within the groups to provide task assistance or to increase students' teamwork skills, and (5) evaluate students' learning and help students process how well their group functioned.

Guidelines for designing formal cooperative learning lesson plans are available in many books and articles, such as Johnson, Johnson, and Smith (2006) and Smith (1996).

Implementation of Cooperative Base Groups. Cooperative base groups are long-term, heterogeneous cooperative learning groups with stable membership whose primary responsibility is to provide each student with the support, encouragement, and assistance he or she needs to make academic progress. Base groups personalize the work required and the course learning experiences. They stay the same during the course and possibly longer. The members of base groups should exchange e-mail addresses and phone numbers and information about schedules because they may wish to meet outside class. When students have successes, insights, questions, or concerns they wish to discuss, they can contact other members of their base group. Base groups typically manage the daily paperwork of the course through the use of group folders or Web-based discussion groups. Base groups are used by many engineering faculty in undergraduate courses and programs, in part because of their effectiveness and because they are easy to implement. They are also commonly used in professional school graduate programs, such as executive master's of business administration and management of technology. In this context, they are usually referred to as cohort groups and are groups of five or six students who stay together during the duration of their graduate program.

Implementation of Problem-Based Learning. Problem-based learning is as suitable for engineering and other STEM disciplines as it is for medicine, where it is used because it helps students develop skills and confidence for formulating problems they have never seen before. This is an important skill, since few STEM professionals are paid to formulate and solve problems that follow from the material presented in the chapter or have a single right answer that one can find at the end of a book.

The intellectual activity of building models to solve problems—an explicit activity of constructing or creating the qualitative or quantitative relationships—helps students understand, explain, and predict (Smith and Starfield, 1993; Starfield, Smith, and Bleloch, 1994). The process of building models together in face-to-face interpersonal interaction results in learning that is difficult to achieve in any other way.

Problem-based learning results from the process of working toward the understanding or resolution of a problem. It follows a learning cycle model: problem posed, identifying learning issues, individual and small group learning, application of learning, and reformulating the problem.

Problem-based learning and, more broadly, challenge-based learning (for example, case-based learning, problem-based learning, project-based learning, and inquiry-based learning) have been described in numerous references and are excellent ways to implement pedagogies of engagement in STEM disciplines. (See Bransford, Vye, and Bateman, 2002, for elaboration on challenge-based learning.)

Conclusion

STEM educators can apply many of the ideas in this chapter to their classroom practices. Increasing the sense of community among STEM students and between students and instructors within STEM classrooms is essential, since cooperative learning researchers and practitioners have shown that positive peer relationships are essential to success in college. Isolation and alienation are the best predictors of failure. Two major reasons for dropping out of college are failure to establish a social network of friends and classmates and failure to become academically involved in classes (Tinto, 1993). Working together with fellow students, solving problems together, and talking through material together have other benefits as well (McKeachie, 1988):

> Student participation, teacher encouragement, and student-student interaction positively relate to improved critical thinking. These three activities confirm other research and theory stressing the importance of active practice, motivation, and feedback in thinking skills as well as other skills. This confirms that discussions . . . are superior to lectures in improving thinking and problem solving [p. 1].

More supportive and engaging learning environments can help us accomplish our most important outcomes for STEM graduates: stronger thinking and reasoning skills, problem formulation and problem-solving skills, skills for working together cooperatively with others, and, especially, skills and confidence for figuring things out in complex environments and situations. We need the courage to relax our coverage compulsion and reach out to engage and involve students in their learning.

References

Anderson, L. W., and Krathwohl, D. R. *A Taxonomy for Learning, Teaching, and Assessing: A Revision of Bloom's Taxonomy of Educational Objectives.* New York: Longman, 2001.

Angelo, T. A., and Cross, K. P. *Classroom Assessment Techniques: A Handbook for College Teachers.* San Francisco: Jossey-Bass, 1993.

Bok, D. *Our Underachieving Colleges: A Candid Look at How Much Students Learn and Why They Should Be Learning More.* Princeton, N.J.: Princeton University Press, 2005.

Bransford, J. D. "Preparing People for Rapidly Changing Environments." *Journal of Engineering Education*, 2007, 96(1), 1–3.

Bransford, J. D., Brown, A. L., and, Cocking, R. R. *How People Learn: Brain, Mind, Experience, and School.* (Exp. ed.) Washington, D.C.: National Academy Press, 2000.

Bransford, J., Vye, N., and Bateman, H. "Creating High-Quality Learning Environments: Guidelines from Research on How People Learn." In P. A. Graham and N. G. Stacey (eds.), *The Knowledge Economy and Postsecondary Education: Report of a Workshop.* Washington, D.C.: National Academy Press, 2002.

Braxton, J. M. (ed.). *Reworking the Student Departure Puzzle.* Nashville, Tenn.: Vanderbilt University, 2000.

Cox, M. F. *An Examination of the Validity of the VaNTH Observation System (VOS).* Nashville, Tenn.: Vanderbilt University, 2005.

Darmofal, D. "Educating the Future: Impact of Pedagogical Reform in Aerodynamics." In D. A. Caughey and M. M. Hafez (eds.), *Computing the Future IV: Frontiers of Computational Fluid Dynamics.* New York: Springer-Verlag, 2005.

Dufresne, R. J., and others. "Classtalk: A Classroom Communication System or Active Learning." *Journal of Computing in Higher Education*, 1996, 7, 3–47.

Fink, L. D. *Creating Significant Learning Experiences: An Integrated Approach to Designing College Courses.* San Francisco: Jossey-Bass, 2003.

Hersh, R. H., and Merrow, J. *Declining by Degrees: Higher Education at Risk.* New York: Palgrave Macmillan, 2005.

Johnson, D. W., and Johnson, F. *Joining Together: Group Theory and Group Skills.* (7th ed.) Needham Heights, Mass.: Allyn and Bacon, 2000.

Johnson, D. W., and Johnson, R. T. *Assessing Students in Groups: Promoting Group Responsibility and Individual Accountability.* Thousand Oaks, Calif.: Corwin, 2004.

Johnson, D. W., Johnson, R. T., and Smith, K. A. "Constructive Controversy: The Power of Intellectual Conflict." *Change,* 2000, *32*(1), 28–37.

Johnson, D. W., Johnson, R. T., and Smith, K. A. *Active Learning: Cooperation in the College Classroom.* (3rd ed.) Edina, Minn.: Interaction Book Company, 2006.

Johnson, D. W., Johnson, R. T., and Smith, K. A. *Active Learning: Cooperation in the College Classroom.* Edina, Minn.: Interaction Book Company, 1998.

Johnson, D. W., Johnson, R. T., and Smith, K. A. "The State of Cooperative Learning in Postsecondary And Professional Settings." *Educational Psychology Review,* 2007, *19*(1), 15–29.

Katzenbach, J. R., and Smith, D. K. *The Wisdom of Teams: Creating the High-performance Organization.* Cambridge, Mass.: Harvard Business School Press, 1993.

Martin, J., Mitchell, J., and Newell, T. "Development of a Concept Inventory for Fluid Mechanics." In *FIE 2003 Conference Proceedings.* Boulder, Colo.: Foundation Coalition, 2003.

Mazur, E. *Peer Instruction: A User's Manual.* Upper Saddle River, N.J.: Prentice Hall, 1997.

McKeachie, W. "From the Associate Director: Teaching Thinking." *National Center for Research to Improve Postsecondary Teaching and Learning—NCRIPTAL Update,* 1988, *2*(1), 1–6.

Mestre, J. P., Gerace, W. J., Dufresne, R. J., and Leonard, W. J. "Promoting Active Learning in Large Classes Using a Classroom Communication System." In E. F. Redish and J. S. Rigden (eds.), *The Changing Role of Physics Departments in Modern Universities: Proceedings of International Conference on Undergraduate Physics Education.* Woodbury, N.Y.: American Institute of Physics, 1997.

National Academy of Sciences, National Academy of Engineering, and Institute of Medicine. *Rising Above the Gathering Storm: Energizing and Employing America for a Brighter Future.* Washington, D.C.: National Academy Press, 2005.

National Science Foundation. *Shaping the Future: New Expectations for Undergraduate Education in Science, Mathematics, Engineering, and Technology.* Arlington, Va.: Director of Education and Human Resources, National Science Foundation, 1996.

Pea, R. D., and Gomez, L. M. "Distributed Multimedia Learning Environments: Why and How?" *Interactive Learning Environments,* 1992, *2,* 73–109.

Pellegrino, J. W. "Rethinking and Redesigning Curriculum, Instruction and Assessment: What Contemporary Research and Theory Suggests." 2006. Retrieved Jan. 5, 2009, from http://www.skillscommission.org/commissioned.htm.

Petrosino, A. J., Martin, T., and Svihla, V. (eds.). *Developing Student Expertise and Community: Lessons from How People Learn.* New Directions for Teaching and Learning, no. 108. San Francisco: Jossey-Bass, 2006.

Roselli, R. J., and Brophy, S. P. "Exploring an Electronic Polling System for the Assessment of Student Progress in Two Biomedical Engineering Courses." In *Proceedings of the American Society for Engineering Education Annual Conference and Exposition.* DEStech Publications, 2002. CD-ROM.

Seymour, E. "Tracking the Processes of Change in US Undergraduate Education in Science, Mathematics, Engineering, and Technology." *Science Education,* 2002, *86,* 79–105.

Seymour, E., and Hewitt, N. M. *Talking About Leaving: Why Undergraduates Leave the Sciences.* Boulder, Colo.: Westview, 1997.

Shuman, L., Besterfield-Sacre, M., and McGourty, J. "The ABET 'Professional Skills'-Can They Be Taught? Can They Be Assessed?" *Journal of Engineering Education,* 2005, *94*(1), 41–56.

Simon, H. A. "Observations on the Sciences of Science Learning." Paper prepared for the Committee on Developments in the Science of Learning for the Sciences of Science

Learning: An Interdisciplinary Discussion, Department of Psychology, Carnegie Mellon University, 1996.

Smith, K. A. "Cooperative Learning: Making 'Groupwork' Work." In C. Bonwell and T. Sutherlund (eds.), *Active Learning: Lessons from Practice and Emerging Issues*. New Directions for Teaching and Learning, no. 67. San Francisco: Jossey-Bass, 1996.

Smith, K. A. "Grading Cooperative Projects." In B. Anderson and B. W. Speck (eds.), *Changing the Way We Grade Student Performance: Classroom Assessment and the New Learning Paradigm*. New Directions for Teaching and Learning, no. 78. San Francisco: Jossey-Bass, 1998.

Smith, K. A., and Imbrie, P. K. *Teamwork and Project Management*. (3rd ed.) New York: McGraw-Hill, 2007.

Smith, K. A., Sheppard, S. D., Johnson, D. W., and Johnson, R. T. "Pedagogies of Engagement: Classroom-Based Practices." *Journal of Engineering Education*, 2005, 94(1), 87–102.

Smith, K. A., and Starfield, A. M. "Building Models to Solve Problems." In J. H. Clarke and A. W. Biddle (eds.), *Teaching Critical Thinking: Reports from Across the Curriculum*. Upper Saddle River, N.J.: Prentice Hall, 1993.

Starfield, A. M., Smith, K. A., and Bleloch, A. L. *How to Model It: Problem Solving for the Computer Age*. Edina, Minn.: Interaction Book Company,1994.

Sullivan, W. M. *Work and Integrity: The Crisis and Promise of Professionalism in America*. San Francisco: Jossey-Bass, 2005.

Tinto, V. "Dropout from Higher Education: A Theoretical Synthesis of Recent Research." *Review of Educational Research*, 1975, 45, 89–125.

Tinto, V. *Leaving College: Rethinking the Causes and Cures of Student Attrition*. Chicago: University of Chicago Press, 1987.

Tinto, V. *Leaving College: Rethinking the Causes and Cures of Student Attrition*. (2nd. ed.) Chicago: University of Chicago Press, 1993.

Wenk L., and others. "Technology-Assisted Active Learning in Large Lectures." In C. D'Avanzo and A. McNichols (eds.), *Student-Active Science: Models of Innovation in College Science Teaching*. Philadelphia: Saunders College, 1997.

Wiggins, G., and McTighe, J. *Understanding by Design*. Alexandria, Va.: Association for Supervision and Curriculum Development, 1998.

KARL A. SMITH *is the Morse-Alumni Distinguished Teaching Professor of Civil Engineering at the University of Minnesota and Cooperative Learning Professor of Engineering Education in the Department of Engineering at Purdue University; he is also editor-in-chief of* Annals of Research on Engineering Education *(AREE).*

TAMEKA CLARKE DOUGLAS *is a Ph.D. student in the School of Engineering Education at Purdue University.*

MONICA F. COX *is an assistant professor in the School of Engineering Education at Purdue University.*

NEW DIRECTIONS FOR TEACHING AND LEARNING • DOI: 10.1002/tl

3

An overlooked role for faculty members in advancing teaching and learning is that of the research advisor who teams with students interested in faculty careers.

Advancing STEM Teaching and Learning with Research Teams

Brian P. Coppola

One of the driving editorial questions for this volume is disconcerting: "Why should faculty members work to enhance undergraduate education?" This is partly because I have an idiosyncratic view on the topic, having built my academic career on an interdisciplinary combination of chemistry and education (Huber, 2004). But mostly the reason is that the answer seems so simple: "It's our job; we are the professors . . . the keepers of the flame of education. . . . If we do not do this, the flame goes out." A more complicated answer is also valid: "Professors have a great deal to do, and our lives are filled with conflicting priorities, increasing demands; one person cannot do everything." Consequently, some familiar solutions to enhancing undergraduate education include outsourcing (hiring some nontenure-track educationalists to take care of this, or even when tenured, at a reduced status), remedial education (consultation with the members of the professional development community who staff the teaching centers), and various forms of denial or bravado ("not my job," "I have important experiments to conduct," "students are just not the same as in the olden days . . ."). And yet in my experience, departments are usually made up of well-intentioned faculty colleagues who sincerely want to do a great job in their classroom teaching, but lack exactly the thing that made them terrific researchers: adequate preparation for the responsibilities of being an independent and creative practitioner.

NEW DIRECTIONS FOR TEACHING AND LEARNING, no. 117, Spring 2009   © Wiley Periodicals, Inc.
Published online in Wiley InterScience (www.interscience.wiley.com) • DOI: 10.1002/tl.342

In this chapter, I begin with something that is nearly self-evident: a primary reason that STEM faculty members are so successful in research, even in the face of constantly changing and exponentially growing information, is the highly intentional program of professional preparation that they receive. For over a hundred years, professional preparation has catapulted individuals who are barely ten to twelve years out of high school to the leading edges of their discipline and provides the sort of readiness that makes them independent and creative practitioners. They are ready to take on and invent new solutions to complex, challenging problems.

The critical component that allows STEM researchers to continue to carry out research even when demands grow and life complicates is the research group: the quid pro quo trade we make to educate the next generation in exchange for getting students to work on our research ideas. Because teaching and learning are areas that intersect every discipline in academia and represent the special dual nature of being a professor (to advance understanding and how we educate), I argue that understanding our system of professional preparation for STEM research is perhaps the best model for how to prepare the future members of the professoriat, but is also exactly what today's professors need in order to get involved with improving undergraduate education.

Preparing the Next Generation for Research

I am compelled by the idea that the most unique and important thing we do, as academic scientists, is identify, nurture, and ultimately move the next generation past what we could accomplish. Our system of scholarly development in research is built on using research as a vehicle for educating students to be the next generation of scholars.

The concept of inherited wisdom is particularly keen in the STEM disciplines because research groups are the norm. As a consequence, ironically enough, the senior member of an academic scientific research team (the faculty advisor) is generally identifiable as the person who does not personally carry out experiments. And if you remove the research students from any science department, it is fair to say that the amount of new knowledge produced would damp to zero in short order. Although it is also fair to say that scientists and engineers have taken the most strategic advantage of the research group, a faculty member such as my colleague Eric Rabkin, a professor of English, has adapted the research group model to take on a problem in analyzing short stories (Genre Evolution Project at the University of Michigan, 2007a).

Roald Hoffmann (private communication, October 2003) believes that research groups, as we know them, are the primary reason that graduate students in the United States hopscotch in creative ability over their better-trained European and Asian counterparts during graduate school. Is this true? We do not know. As a mid-twentieth-century phenomenon, large academic research groups have been studied as organizational structures by only a few educational researchers (Lave and Wenger, 1991; Latour, 1987;

NEW DIRECTIONS FOR TEACHING AND LEARNING • DOI: 10.1002/tl

Latour and Woolgar, 1991; Goodwin, 1995; Newstetter, 2005). Much more work is needed to understand research groups, because they are an important mechanism by which the intellectual and social "genes" for learning about scholarship (what Dawkins, 1989, calls memes) are inherited.

Research groups are the nuclear families of academia, and the obligation we have to replace ourselves in academia is profound. If academic scientists stopped doing research, discoveries would still be made. If academic scientists stopped filing patents, inventions would still be invented. But if academic scientists stopped educating the next generation of academics, the entire system of educating scientists comes to a swift and grinding halt.

We owe it to the next generation to educate as well as possible, and my thesis is that integrating a scholarly development model in teaching and learning—for all of those who become the next generation of academics, based on what we know from research—is the necessary next step in the evolution of our profession.

Preparation for Teaching

In arguing for a "broader, more capacious meaning" of scholarship (Boyer, 1990; Glassick, Huber, and Maeroff, 1997), Boyer and his colleagues proposed that in addition to a scholarship of discovery (that is, the tenets of scholarship as applied to research), there could be a scholarship of teaching and learning (SoTL). The SoTL community comprises a widespread group of faculty members, administrators, and personnel from college and university teaching centers (Indiana University, 2007).

Randy Bass, in a seminal 1999 article, provides what I think is a powerful litmus test for the existence proof of a scholarship of teaching and learning. One telling measure of how differently teaching is regarded from traditional scholarship or research within the academy is what a difference it makes to have a "problem" in one versus the other. In scholarship and research, having a "problem" is at the heart of the investigative process; it is the compound of the generative questions around which all creative and productive activity revolves. But in one's teaching, a "problem" is something you don't want to have, and if you have one, you probably want to fix it. Asking a colleague about a problem in his or her research is an invitation; asking about a problem in one's teaching would probably seem like an accusation.

In other words, we readily differentiate between the meaning of the word *problem* in the following two phrases: "my research problem" and "a problem with my research." In the first case, we mean a project in which we are investing our scholarly energy, into which we welcome students and faculty collaborators in an intellectual pursuit. In the second case, the sense of the word *problem* shifts to a difficulty that needs to be fixed. When you quite literally swap the word *teaching* for the word *research* in those phrases, the dual meaning of the word *problem* disappears. We read and understand "my teaching problem" as synonymous with "a problem with my teaching."

New Directions for Teaching and Learning • DOI: 10.1002/tl

Language is revealing. A scholarship of teaching and learning will not exist, I believe, until we have language (and therefore the idea) that differentiates the meaning of the two "teaching" phrases to the same degree that we differentiate the two "research" phrases.

If the meaning of scholarship is broad and capacious, then, as a first approximation, the "teaching" for "research" swap can be used to help clarify what a scholarship of teaching and learning looks like. By studying and describing the characteristics of scholarship that we understand so well from research, we can then quite literally read how the tenets of scholarship suggest what is needed to advance teaching and learning. In the following statements, which were originally a set of four characteristics of scholarship in research (Coppola, 2007), I have used the "Bass substitution strategy" to generate statements for the characteristics of scholarship in teaching and learning:

- *Scholarship in teaching and learning means that the work is informed.* A teacher should know as much as is knowable about the problem, how to search that information out, how the problem fits into the overall needs and interests of the teaching community, and how to evaluate the scope and limitations of the teaching methods that were used to generate the resulting knowledge. A teacher understands the standards of practice that affect the design of a project, including critical issues of intellectual property, authorship, ethical conduct, and resolution of conflicts.
- *Scholarship in teaching and learning means that the work is intentional.* A teacher should be able to link explicitly, or align, the informed goals of a project with the methods being used to implement it, and to have defensible arguments for why these choices will result in the expected knowledge gains. A teacher should provide multiple and reliable sources of evaluation data that address directly the goals set out by the teaching objectives and the methods used to implement the teaching design.
- *Scholarship in teaching and learning means understanding that the model is impermanent.* Teachers understand that their contributions are tentative and theory laden, and the new questions that arise from their teaching will make the work itself a target for falsification. The decreasing half-life of information has significant consequences for the lives of academic teachers, or, said more plainly, it is not so much that we are eliminating the flat earth model as much as we are creating the next best version of it. Only intellectual arrogance makes us think that we have finally found a single, immutable answer to anything. The phenomena (motivation, cognition, creativity, and so forth) remain, but at any moment, the model is open to evolution or revolution. Understanding impermanence can keep teachers critical about their own work and less inclined toward conservative critics who say, "Science teaching progresses funeral by funeral."
- *Scholarship in teaching and learning means that both results and processes are inheritable.* Teachers provide the kind of documentation of their work

NEW DIRECTIONS FOR TEACHING AND LEARNING • DOI: 10.1002/tl

that allows other teachers to evaluate it without having looked over the shoulder of the practitioner. A teacher's body of work exists in forms that can be shared, learned from, and built on. However, there is much more to the process of becoming a teacher who follows the tenets of scholarship than having access to a good library. All of the characteristics of scholarship . . . work that is informed, intentional, and documented and acknowledges impermanence . . . need to be learned, too. And as with most things, explicit and deliberate instruction is better than implicit and haphazard instruction.

Building Teaching Groups on the Experience of Building Research Groups

Faculty members in the laboratory sciences currently develop their teaching ideas quite differently than they do their research ideas. In fact, they carry out teaching projects the same way a historian does research: alone. Yet particularly in science, we successfully involve inexperienced students in our discovery research plans, using a system that engages potential researchers as early as their entry into college, and one that continues to move them along through the end of their postdoctoral period. That same system should, hypothetically, engage those students who want to add education, along with science, to their professional preparation—not all students but rather that subset interested in academic careers.

Working on large, team-based projects is not a priori limited to scientific research just because science caught that particular wave when the tide of public funding came in. As a strategy to improve professional readiness for future faculty members, building teaching groups from the personnel in our research groups, and taking on the teaching missions of our departments, serves everyone. As academics, attending to the best possible professional readiness for those who become professors is our unique and key obligation; our only choice is how well (or badly) we do it.

To enhance undergraduate education, we need to combine faculty members, and their big ideas about research and teaching, with the students who want to add this combination to their education: the future faculty. In my department, building teaching groups started by following the Bass substitution strategy: the things we do to promote professional readiness for research already exist (Coppola and Roush, 2004; Coppola, 2007). Over the past ten years, if the question was, "How do we handle this for doing teaching projects?" then we have learned that the first, best answer is, "Let's take a look at what we already do in research and create an analogy." In the abstract, this means:

1. Thinking about instructional design that will not only identify students for their potential as researchers, but also for their potential as teachers

NEW DIRECTIONS FOR TEACHING AND LEARNING • DOI: 10.1002/tl

2. Thinking more expansively about what you ask students to do in a course because you are going to partner with your instructors-in-training on your teaching ideas in the same way you partner with your researchers-in-training on your research ideas
3. Thinking through what parts of a project can be implemented by undergraduate collaborators, graduate collaborators, and postdoctoral collaborators
4. Working with people outside your areas of expertise in order to innovate with instructional design or to collect and understand assessment data
5. Providing course work and seminars for students in areas of education
6. Finding fellowship support for Ph.D. students and postdoctoral associates, because that is how we operate in general when we carry out interdisciplinary work
7. Embracing that all of the participants are still first and foremost (in my department) chemists, and not a separate or segregated subset of faculty members and students who are the educationalists, but rather that subset of mainstream scientists in the department who want to add this work to their portfolio
8. Having, in the first iteration, one or two faculty members who can take leadership for organizing and administering this activity within the department

A decade later, we have made progress. When my colleagues think about doing instructional development, they think about partnering with students in order to get that work done (Gottfried and others, 2007). We have sections of our first-year courses where the instruction is deliberately designed to help reveal both disciplinary expertise and the ability to teach along with creating instructional materials (Hayward and Coppola, 2005; Varma-Nelson and Coppola, 2005). Our colleagues in the University of Michigan School of Education have adapted some of their graduate courses so that postsecondary education is featured along with precollege science education, and our graduate students take these courses. We have used funding from the U.S. Department of Education's GAANN program (Graduate Assistantships in Areas of National Need) to support graduate students (as one might with a training grant) who wanted to add significant work in education to their chemistry Ph.D. program, and a number of these students have included chapters on their scholarship of teaching and learning in their written theses. In fall 2007, we had eight postdoctoral associates in the department whose primary residency was in one of the department's research groups, into which they had been recruited, but who also held a mentored teaching assignment as an instructor in one of our courses—generally, but not always, as part of a multiperson team in the introductory program.

NEW DIRECTIONS FOR TEACHING AND LEARNING • DOI: 10.1002/tl

Reflections on the Program

In 2003, I invited Janet Lawrence, a faculty member in our Center for the Study of Higher and Post-Secondary Education (University of Michigan, 2007b), to carry out a review of our program. We had three overriding questions: (1) Was there evidence that graduate students participating in our program were becoming better educated about concerns and issues related to education? (2) Was there evidence that graduate students participating in our program were more aware of concerns and issues related to faculty careers? and (3) Was there evidence that the department had embraced this program as a core part of its mission? The results were all positive. It is unusual for a large research department to bring education on teaching and learning into its central mission, and one of the common questions we got early on was, "I can see how this might be accepted once it is established, but how did it get there?" William Roush, the department chair at the time, gave perhaps the best answer: "six hundred thousand dollars in graduate fellowships per year and a competitive advantage for recruiting graduate students and new faculty members creates lots of agnostics. . . . They might not be believers, but they are not willing to get out the torches and pitchforks either . . . ."

There is a lesson here worth reflecting on about change. As a strategy, providing resources that attract faculty participation, in their familiar role as faculty advisors, appears to be much more effective than scolding them because of what they are not doing as well as you think they might.

My colleagues and I are certainly not alone in these efforts, although we think our plan is both philosophically and qualitatively different from other approaches. There is work across the country that can be interpreted as using one or more of the four characteristics of scholarship to engage students and faculty in teaching and learning. Undergraduate peer-led instructional programs speak directly to student engagement (Varma-Nelson and Coppola, 2005). At the graduate level, there are a large number of Preparing Future Faculty (PFF) programs (Preparing Future Faculty, 2007). Chemistry and physics departments that offer Ph.D.s in chemistry or physics education are carrying out informed and credible research (Coppola and Jacobs, 2002).

The PFF Program, in great part, was a response to the reports and concerns of young faculty and graduate students (Caserio and others, 2004; Golde and Dore, 2004) on whom expectations were rising but for whom there were diminishing resources. One of the important rationales for PFF programs was the fact that only 6 percent of schools grant doctoral degrees, so, by definition, the sort of school where a Ph.D. is likely to get an academic position is unlike the place where the doctorate was earned. In general, PFF programs expose students to the significantly different settings and concerns where the majority of higher education takes place. Although there is no single response to PFF programs, a caricature of the first reactions heard from the established STEM faculty is: "I did not need this, and I am a good teacher, why should they?" or "Nothing's broken. What are you trying to fix?" or "There is plenty done for young faculty once they start their careers." You get the idea.

PFF programs have raised the level of consciousness about improving professional readiness. However, with some exceptions, PFF is a marginalized activity and tends to be centralized administratively rather than in departments. There are too many stories of students in PFF programs who keep their participation below the radar for fear of retaliation from their advisors for being away from their research. The PFF curriculum is generally divided between administrative units (such as a graduate school) and the non-Ph.D.-granting partner schools; so, and I am critical here, mainstream faculty members have outsourced the "learning about teaching" part of their responsibilities. Perhaps not surprisingly, the national review (Boylan, 2003) found that PFF had had only moderate impact on change in either the core Ph.D.-granting departments and, interestingly enough, even less on the partnering departments.

Reflections on Current Practices

Over the years, I have worked with many of the people and organizations that have been concerned with improving higher education. These interactions have helped shape my thinking. Far from a critique, I want to provide brief reflections on the five efforts that, in my view, comprise the main landscape for thinking about teaching and learning in the United States. And as with all general characterizations, there are better and worse examples than the caricature, but I am attempting here to capture a general impression. Of course, these are my own impressions as someone looking into these initiatives. The leaders of these programs and efforts might describe them differently.

Professional and Organizational Development. The typical place where you find professional and organizational development (POD) activity is in a campus's center for teaching excellence or whatever it is called locally (POD Network, 2007). These organizations recognize that faculty members hit the ground of their new positions underprepared, and the staff of these centers provide much-needed intervention and service. While POD staff recognize that faculty members are the incomplete product of a flawed system, there is a tendency, in my view, to treat faculty members as students. And by treating faculty members as students and waiting until the start of one's professional appointment, the POD approach may inadvertently advance the "I have a teaching problem" mentality and does not address solutions for the flaws in the system that gave rise to the need for teaching centers in the first place. Finding ways for faculty members to take on responsibilities that are more like their work as research advisors taps into a quite different mind-set for thinking about education.

Scholarship of Teaching and Learning Community. The scholarship of teaching and learning (SoTL) initiatives has inspired mainstream faculty members to think about reflective practice and to treat one's individual activity in the classroom as an object of inquiry (Indiana University, 2007). And yet the SoTL community has wrestled with its relationship to the education research community since the outset. In the first issue of the *International Journal on the Scholarship of Teaching and Learning* (Georgia Southern University, 2007), the opening essay by Pat Hutchings focuses on the growth of using educational theory (and other theories) as a basis for carrying out classroom research. Nearly all of the articles in this issue, gathered in a section titled "Research," are indistinguishable from the papers one might find in education research journals. Does the scholarship of teaching and learning reduce to the subset of educational research when your own class is the object of the research? What is missing from these articles is any sense of faculty members who are teaching their subject and making teaching choices informed by work that aligns their instructional goals and methods. The scholarship of teaching and learning is too often used only as a noun; as a thing that is being done rather than an overall process.

The Ph.D. in the Disciplinary Education Community. This group fills a significant void in many schools of education where there is no research focus on postsecondary teaching and learning. In my discipline, and I know it is true for others, there is an unfortunate tendency for this group of faculty to see themselves as the self-appointed "chemical educators," and an even more unfortunate tendency for the rest of the faculty to think that this is just fine (Coppola and Jacobs, 2002). Two-tier faculty systems are intrinsically problematic. More than that, I cannot support a system that dissociates and absolves people who are called professors from their responsibilities as educators. Advancing the profession derives from individuals who possess a deeply integrated understanding of the subject and its pedagogy (Shulman, 1986; Magnusson, Krajcik, and Borko, 1999).

The Teaching-as-Research Community. This group recognizes the need to engage graduate students and faculty members together on projects that use research-based skills to examine and improve teaching and learning (University of Wisconsin, 2007a). As such, it shares many attributes with the SoTL community. The program has assembled extensive bibliographies on topics such as using diversity to enhance learning. The bulk of the investment is in workshops and classes at member institutions and now across the network of member universities. As with PFF and SoTL, the open concern is the degree to which large numbers of STEM faculty are deeply involved in the work and the extent to which graduate students' interest in developing as teachers is supported or marginalized by their faculty advisors.

The Adapt-and-Adopt Community. "Adapt and adopt" is a term used by the National Science Foundation (NSF) for its dissemination practices. NSF encourages the development of teaching materials that are relatively "teacher proof," or, in their lingo, "robust deliverables." I think robust deliverables are good—but also not so good. An important community of people has worked hard to make active classroom practices, as an example, accessible to faculty members who were otherwise treating classrooms as a place to deliver seminars. Personal responses systems, peer-led team learning (City College of New York, 2007), process-oriented guided inquiry learning (POGIL, 2007), and so on, many of which are the stepchildren of Angelo and Cross's classroom assessment techniques (1993) have actually changed practices. This is terrific. Unfortunately, from my point of view, there can be a methodological evangelism that does not care to link, or align, specific learning goals with a rationale for why understanding the subject matter will improve when these methods are used. That is, with this strategy, I have observed well-intentioned faculty who think about education as a trip to the supermarket to see what new products there are to pull from the shelf.

Conclusion

Improving and enhancing higher education is an irresistible force because it is, in the end, our job. And yet when this force hits the immovable objects of the twenty-four-hour day and conflicting work priorities, education efforts have generally ended up splintering . . . . Cuban (1999) would say they were trumped . . . by incrementally growing demands to maintain research competitiveness. My view, which I have outlined in this chapter, is that we can do both by changing the way we do our work. In order to take on substantive research, STEM faculty learned that the twenty-four-hour-day barrier could be overcome by becoming more efficient. Research groups accomplish the twin goals of being able to organize a significant research effort while we ensure that the next generation of researchers inherits what we know and does not end up needing to reinvent those things. The features of that system are missing from teaching and learning, where faculty members inherit literally nothing about what is known and, as Cuban (1990) also rightly points out, end up "reforming . . . again, again and again" (p. 3). Cuban concludes that "waves [of reform] occur on the surface [of formal education] and, in some instances, programs, like the skeletons of long-dead sea animals, get deposited on the coral reef of schooling . . . [yet reform itself goes critically unexamined]. . . . I end with a plea for rationality. . . . If we do not heed the plea, we will continue to mindlessly speculate, and as Gide observed: Everything has been said before, but since nobody listens, we have to keep going back and begin again" (p. 12). I agree.

References

Angelo, T., and Cross, K. P. *Classroom Assessment Techniques.* San Francisco: Jossey-Bass, 1993.

Bass, R. "The Scholarship of Teaching: What's the Problem?" *Inventio,* 1999, *1*(1). Retrieved Mar. 23, 2007, from http://www.doit.gmu.edu/inventio/issues/Spring_1999/Bass_1.html.

Boyer, E. L. *Scholarship Reconsidered: Priorities of the Professoriate.* Princeton, N.J.: Carnegie Foundation for the Advancement of Teaching, 1990.

Boylan, M. "Evaluation of the PFF Program." CIRTL Annual Forum, Madison, Wis., Nov. 2003. Retrieved Mar. 23, 2007, from http://cirtl.wceruw.org/Forum2003/speaker_presentations.html.

Caserio, M., and others. "Responses to Changing Needs in U.S. Doctoral Education." *Journal of Chemical Education,* 2004, *81,* 1698–1705.

Coppola, B. P. "The Most Beautiful Theories." *Journal of Chemical Education,* 2007, *84,* 1902–1911.

Coppola, B. P., and Jacobs, D. "Is the Scholarship of Teaching and Learning New to Chemistry?" In M. T. Huber and S. Morreale (eds.), *Disciplinary Styles in the Scholarship of Teaching and Learning: A Conversation.* Washington, D.C.: American Association of Higher Education and Carnegie Foundation for the Advancement of Teaching, 2002.

Coppola, B. P., and Roush, W. R. "Broadening the Existing Intergenerational Structure of Scholarly Development in Chemistry." *Peer Review,* 2004, *6*(3), 19–21.

Cuban, L. "Reforming Again, Again, and Again." *Educational Researcher,* 1990, *19,* 3–13.

Cuban, L. *How Scholars Trumped Teachers: Change Without Reform in University Curriculum, Teaching, and Research, 1890–1990.* New York: Teachers College Press, 1999.

Dawkins, R. *The Selfish Gene.* (New ed.) New York: Oxford University Press, 1989.

Georgia Southern University. "Theory: The Elephant in the Scholarship of Teaching and Learning Room." Jan. 2007. Retrieved Mar. 23, 2007, from http://www.georgiasouthern.edu/ijsotl/.

Glassick, C. E., Huber, M. T., and Maeroff, G. I. *Scholarship Assessed: Evaluation of the Professoriate.* San Francisco: Jossey-Bass, 1997.

Golde, C. M., and Dore, T. M. "The Survey of Doctoral Education and Career Preparation: The Importance of Disciplinary Contexts." In D. H. Wulff, A. E. Austin, and Associates (eds.), *Path to the Professoriate: Strategies for Enriching the Preparation of Future Faculty.* San Francisco: Jossey-Bass, 2004.

Goodwin, C. "Seeing in Depth." *Social Studies of Science,* 1995, *25,* 237–274.

Gottfried, A. C., and others. "Design and Implementation of a Studio-Based General Chemistry Course at the University of Michigan." *Journal of Chemical Education,* 2007, *84,* 265–270.

Hayward, L. M., and Coppola, B. P. "Teaching and Technology: Making the Invisible Explicit and Progressive Through Reflection." *Journal of Physical Therapy Education,* 2005, *19*(3), 30–40.

Huber, M. T. *Balancing Acts: The Scholarship of Teaching and Learning in Academic Careers.* Washington, D.C.: American Association for Higher Education and Carnegie Foundation for the Advancement of Teaching, 2004.

Latour, B. *Science in Action.* Cambridge, Mass.: Harvard University Press, 1987.

Latour, B., and Woolgar, S. *Laboratory Life: The Construction of Scientific Facts.* Princeton, N.J.: Princeton University Press, 1991.

Lave, J., and Wenger, E. *Situated Learning: Legitimate Peripheral Participation.* Cambridge: Cambridge University Press, 1991.

Magnusson, S., Krajcik, J., and Borko, H. "Nature, Sources, and Development of Pedagogical Content Knowledge for Science Teaching." In J. Gess-Newsome and N. Lederman (eds.), *Examining Pedagogical Content Knowledge: The Construct and Its Implications for Science Education.* Norwell, Mass.: Kluwer, 1999.

Newstetter, W. "Designing Cognitive Apprenticeships in Biomedical Engineering." *Journal of Engineering Education,* 2005, *94*(2), 207–213.

Shulman, L. S. "Those Who Understand: Knowledge Growth in Teaching." *Educational Researcher,* 1986, *15*(2), 4–14.

University of Michigan. "Genre Evolution Project." 2007a. Retrieved Mar. 23, 2007, from http://www.umich.edu/~genreevo/.
University of Michigan. Unpublished document. 2007b. Retrieved Mar. 23, 2007, from http://www.soe.umich.edu/cshpe/.
Varma-Nelson, P., and Coppola, B. P. "Team Learning." In N. Pienta, M. M. Cooper, and T. Greenbowe (eds.), *Chemist's Guide to Effective Teaching*. Upper Saddle River, N.J.: Pearson, 2005.

BRIAN P. COPPOLA is Arthur F. Thurnau Professor of Chemistry and associate chair for curriculum and faculty affairs in the Department of Chemistry at the University of Michigan, Ann Arbor. He is the codirector of the IDEA (Instructional Development and Educational Assessment) Institute.

NEW DIRECTIONS FOR TEACHING AND LEARNING • DOI: 10.1002/tl

4

This chapter describes insights gained in the College of Engineering at Penn State in implementing collegewide, department-focused, and faculty-centered educational reforms.

Facilitating Reforms in STEM Undergraduate Education: An Administrative Perspective

Thomas A. Litzinger, Richard J. Koubek, David N. Wormley

One of the most important elements in achieving significant curricular and pedagogical innovation is creating a climate that promotes and acknowledges the contributions of those who engage in these efforts. It is critical that this climate be systemic, existing at the department, college, and university levels.

In the past few years, the view that both what we teach and how we teach are of vital importance has shed some new light on what is required to achieve a sustainable and significant improvement in the way students learn (Bransford, Brown, and Cocking, 2000). Creating an environment in which faculty draw on the significant educational research that is relevant to the challenges and opportunities of STEM (science, technology, engineering, and mathematics) undergraduate education is a major factor in successful reform.

There are a number of barriers to establishing a climate in which substantial reform can occur, including a lack of acknowledgment and reward for faculty who undertake curricular reform and the fact that major curriculum reform requires substantial effort and time. There are, however, also a number of imperatives that require that reform of STEM undergraduate education be undertaken:

New Directions for Teaching and Learning, no. 117, Spring 2009 © Wiley Periodicals, Inc.
Published online in Wiley InterScience (www.interscience.wiley.com) • DOI: 10.1002/tl.343

- External global competitive pressures that demand the United States pro- duce the very best STEM graduates (National Academy of Sciences, National Academy of Engineering, and Institute of Medicine, 2005)
- Pressures from professional and accreditation organizations that require extensive assessment of programs and preparation of graduates who can directly enter the workplace fully prepared to contribute
- The rapid change in technology, which has allowed new modes of learn- ing and ways of engaging students to deepen understanding
- Competitive pressures from peer institutions as new and innovative pro- grams are developed that reflect future technological needs
- The fact that a small percentage of U.S. students, particularly students from underrepresented groups, are attracted to STEM undergraduate edu- cation programs (National Science Board, 2006)

These imperatives provide strong motivation for universities, colleges, and departments that wish to be viewed as leaders to develop curricula and learning experiences to educate students who can truly make an impact in the future.

The curriculum reform process has been the topic of numerous stud- ies (Sunal and others, 2001; Seymour, 2002; Clark, Froyd, Merton, and Richardson, 2004). In this chapter, we do not review this body of scholarly work. Rather, we share some of our experiences in undertaking curriculum and pedagogical reforms that have been collegewide and department focused, as well as faculty centered.

Collegewide Reform

Collegewide curriculum reform requires significant effort to establish a cli- mate that supports and encourages reform. Leadership by the dean as well as buy-in from departments within a college are critical. Many organiza- tions, when undertaking such reform, have used a retreat of critical mem- bers of a college, including leading faculty, department heads, and the deans, to identify the rationale for undertaking reform and to broadly sketch out the essential parameters of the reform. Committees are then often formed to undertake the detailed design of new curricula and peda- gogical approaches. To undertake significant curriculum reform, it is imper- ative that there be a strong and continuing commitment from the senior leadership, widespread involvement of the faculty in decision making, and access to the necessary resources, both financial and intellectual, to support and implement the reform.

In engineering colleges, a number of characteristics have been impor- tant drivers in the development of new curricula and new approaches to learning. One significant factor at a number of major public institutions is the retention rate of engineering students, which borders on 50 percent and may be even lower for groups underrepresented in engineering. Although

NEW DIRECTIONS FOR TEACHING AND LEARNING • DOI: 10.1002/tl

there is full realization that as students begin their college career they must explore and determine what programs are best matched to their capabilities and interests, the low retention rate for engineering programs led to an assessment of the impact of the curriculum on retention.

In the 1990s, findings from two highly influential studies of why students leave engineering and the sciences were published (Hewitt and Seymour, 1992; Astin, 1993). These studies revealed that some of the most significant reasons were loss of interest, the prospect of a "better education" in a nontechnical major, and poor teaching quality. The findings of these studies provided a strong impetus to make changes in engineering curricula to boost student interest and improve teaching quality. One of the most common changes undertaken was the introduction of engineering experiences for students in their first and second years. These efforts have taken many forms, including first-year design courses, first-year seminars, and other experiences to allow students to become familiar with engineering principles and the creative aspects of engineering early in their studies. In addition, there have been significant efforts devoted to improving the learning climate for students (Felder, Felder, and Dietz, 1998; Fromm, 2003). These efforts have included more effectively using technology as well as developing in faculty a better understanding of factors that influence the ability of students to learn (Olds and Miller, 2004). The overall success of these changes in the curriculum remains to be fully evaluated in a formal manner. However, initial assessment results have indicated that these types of collegewide curricula changes have had a positive influence on the retention of engineering students.

These efforts have a common thread. First, a significant, documented, negative impact of the curriculum was identified, in this case, poor retention of undergraduate students. Second, based on this information, a strong case could be made that faculty and administrators need to address this issue. Third, steps were identified and implemented to address this issue. Finally, assessment processes were initiated to measure the effectiveness of the changes. It is critical that as reforms are undertaken, specific plans for assessment and evaluation are formulated. Such assessment must ultimately determine what students have learned and whether what they have learned had an important impact in their careers.

Department-Focused Reform

We begin this section with a case study about a major curriculum reform effort in the Marcus Department of Industrial and Manufacturing Engineering (IME) at Penn State. Following the discussion of the case, we highlight the key lessons learned in this process.

Case Study: Reforming the Manufacturing Curriculum. During the mid-1980s and early 1990s, the IME targeted manufacturing as a key area of growth and investment. Distinguished professors and resources followed, as did orientation of the undergraduate curriculum. Since that time,

NEW DIRECTIONS FOR TEACHING AND LEARNING • DOI: 10.1002/tl

outsourcing of manufacturing in the United States has rapidly changed the very nature of work performed by industrial engineers, requiring a curriculum reoriented to the new balance between manufacturing and service sectors of the economy. Based on feedback from alumni, employers, and students, three primary changes were needed: modification of the curriculum to better prepare students for jobs in the service sector, evolution of the focus of manufacturing courses from traditional processes to contemporary ones, and introduction of experiential learning throughout the curriculum.

While the need for change was clear, two unsuccessful attempts at curriculum reform had occurred in the past ten years, experiences that left many members of the IME faculty doubting that another attempt would be worthwhile. Fortunately, over the past few years, several faculty members had been involved in course-specific enhancements. In one case, a team of five faculty members received funding from the Leonhard Center at Penn State to create a team-taught two-course sequence that incorporates experiential learning in a project-based, two-semester class (Simpson and others, 2004). Using these course-specific examples of reform already completed, the case could be made that change certainly was possible. Those with experience in course reform agreed, and ultimately the faculty elected to try one more time.

Rather than struggling to get off the mark, the department was able to leverage existing curricular leadership at the college level. The Leonhard Center Advisory Board, composed of successful alumni, created a model of a World Class Engineer that included a list of critical attributes. This model was endorsed by the dean and provided the benchmark by which the department could measure the current curriculum and identify target areas for change.

Faculty who had been involved with the Leonhard Center in the past viewed it as a respected resource. Consequently, they were open to having the center director serve as an external consultant during the change process. He spoke to the faculty about experiential learning, discussed curriculum reform, and helped everyone understand the issues in the change process.

In previous reform attempts, the proposals had been created by a representative subgroup of faculty, in consultation with the full faculty, and were ultimately presented to the faculty body for approval. This time, an effort was made to include all faculty members early on so they would have direct input in creating the final proposal. To this end, the full faculty decided on how many credit hours would be allocated to each of the four areas within IE. From this determination, each faculty member was assigned to one of the areas, and these teams were required to bring forth a proposal on how to best use these credit hours. An oversight committee consisting of one representative from each area met regularly to ensure coordination and address the common courses. In this manner, all were engaged in working on innovative ways to enhance their particular area.

Once the subgroups had completed the recommendations for their curriculum component, the recommendations were brought back before the full faculty for a vote. In three of the four cases, the subgroup members all agreed, and their proposals easily passed the full faculty. However, one group split along philosophical lines and could not agree, threatening to stop the whole process. When it was clear that there would be no compromise, the faculty as a whole asked for curriculum proposals representing both approaches. Presentations were made for each position, and a vote was taken. The final full proposal was able to move forward.

Extensive faculty energy was invested in the curriculum change process. There were hallway discussions, the reform became the topic of conversation at faculty meetings, and the conference rooms were in high demand as groups were meeting continuously. While necessary, this level of activity was quite time-consuming. Both the department head and dean emphasized the importance of this project and reassured the faculty that their efforts would be recognized.

A major reform of the IME curriculum was ultimately passed. It aligns with the college's vision of a World Class Engineer, contains course tracks in service enterprise engineering and information systems, incorporates a completely new set of courses for the manufacturing component, includes experiential learning through case studies in the nonlaboratory courses, and sets the stage for including modifications in the future. Although the final curriculum looks different from what was anticipated at the outset, these differences are for the better. The department is using existing assessment processes related to accreditation and focus groups with students to begin assessing the overall impact of the reforms.

Lessons Learned. Department heads hold a unique position as the translator and intermediary among the students, faculty, the college, and the university. When curriculum reforms are undertaken, this unique position places the department head at the heart of the change process. The successful reform process described in the case study has provided a number of important lessons for department heads about managing the change process:

- *Identify and support a core group of committed faculty.* In the early stages, there will be faculty who are committed to curricular reform and passionate about the need. They may perceive a political risk in leading a charge for changing status quo. This group (and the full faculty) should sense the department head's unwavering commitment and full support for curricular reform.
- *Engage the entire faculty.* Nobody can sit on the sidelines. In a major curricular reform, the full faculty should be active in some manner. Early on, the department head will thoughtfully determine how this is to occur. In a larger faculty, everybody cannot be engaged in all discussions; hence, the head may choose to partition the reform into components and have subgroups work on these elements. Regardless of how

reform is accomplished, all should have a voice and also carry responsibility for its success.

- *Plan on being flexible.* As the reform discussions unfold, it may very well evolve from what the head had originally envisioned. Everyone should be prepared for this evolution, given the dynamic, recursive nature of the process. Provided the fundamental tenets are accomplished, being adaptive is key.

- *Take a stand at the impasse.* During this process, even after compromises, the group may come to an impasse. The head carries responsibility to ensure the process does not derail. It should be clear to all that abandoning the process is not an option. Communicating and seeking counsel with the dean at points such as these can provide a fresh perspective and the support needed to see the process through.

- *Understand the costs.* A major curricular reform is costly in terms of time, energy, and finances. Resources will be needed to execute the course changes proposed. A head should speak frankly about this at the beginning with both the faculty and dean's office. Also, a definitive time line for completion should be provided so faculty members know a conclusion is in sight.

- *Engage the experts.* Ideally the college or university will have individuals who are experts in teaching science and engineering. Request that these people serve as consultants throughout the process. Ask them to speak at a faculty meeting. Refer to them when necessary, and keep them in the loop as needed.

- *Align the department activities with the college priorities.* It should be clear among the faculty that the department is part of a college activity, and the dean's office is both aware and supportive of the direction. The head holds responsibility for communicating with the dean on directions of the department and conveying to the faculty how the program fits within the larger college vision.

- *Assess the changes.* Given that the process of change is continuous, set key milestones and assess progress toward the goal and the overall impact of the changes.

Faculty-Centered Changes

Changes in curricula, course content, or pedagogical methods ultimately rely on changes enacted by individual faculty members. Such changes are often undertaken by faculty members who are intrinsically motivated to seek the necessary knowledge and resources to bring about the changes they desire. For many other faculty members, however, the press of their multiple responsibilities in research, teaching, and service and their personal priorities does not allow them to invest the time necessary to implement changes without additional support. For a number of universities in the

United States, teaching and learning centers are a common approach to providing this support (Cross, 2001).

Singer (2002) notes that the responsibilities of such centers are shifting away from remediation of poor teaching to assisting instructors in implementing alternative pedagogical approaches, including technology-based teaching and learning in all their myriad forms. Such centers also facilitate access to relevant findings from the cognitive and learning sciences. In addition, due to the increasing importance placed on assessment by accreditation organizations, teaching and learning centers are now being asked to assist individual faculty members, departments, and colleges in learning about and implementing assessment processes.

Typically the teaching and learning centers serve the entire university; however, such centers are also found within specific colleges, perhaps most commonly in colleges of engineering. The Center for the Advancement of Scholarship in Engineering Education (2006) at the National Academy of Engineering lists fifteen such centers in the United States. At Penn State, the Leonhard Center for the Enhancement of Engineering Education was formed in 1990 as a result of a gift from an alumnus. The center provides substantial resources, including financial support, to assist departments in the process of change. The next two case studies describe the roles that the center has played in enacting faculty-centered changes.

Case Study: Integrating Ethics into Engineering Classes. A successful faculty-centered activity has been implemented to enable engineering faculty members to integrate ethics into their classes (Litzinger and others, 2003). The need for enhanced education in ethics was identified through assessment processes related to accreditation of our undergraduate programs. Once the need was identified, the director of the Leonhard Center began a process of formulating a strategy to meet the need in collaboration with the director of the Ethics Institute in the College of the Liberal Arts. Together the two directors and three other faculty members from engineering and philosophy created a model for a one-week summer workshop that was strongly influenced by the long-standing workshop provided by Michael Davis at the Illinois Institute of Technology (Davis, 1999).

Participants in the workshop committed to spend a week of their summer in the workshop and received one week of summer salary. More important, they all committed to design new elements that would integrate ethics into their classes and implement those elements in the upcoming academic year. They gave their permission for assessment of the impact of their ethics activities and committed to attend an end-of-the-year meeting to discuss their progress. During the workshop, participants were engaged in one-day primers on ethical frameworks and a systematic instructional design process. During the third day of the workshop, they were introduced to resource materials from the literature on ethics education and related assessment tools, and then they began designing their new course elements. After an interlude of several weeks, the participants reassembled to present their designs to the group and receive feedback and suggestions for improvements. The workshop has been offered four times and has reached more than thirty faculty members in engineering, more than 10 percent of the college faculty. The courses in which the participants integrated their ethics activities reach more than a thousand students annually.

Case Study: Implementing Pedagogical Reforms. The second case study is an ongoing program to engage faculty members in the use of Tablet-PCs in their classes. Faculty interest in the TabletPC became apparent after they realized its capabilities to enhance teaching from its use in the ethics workshop and a faculty orientation workshop. TabletPCs provide professors in a field such as engineering with the opportunity to devote more class time to active learning activities during class because the lecture portion can proceed more efficiently. TabletPCs also make possible novel strategies for instruction outside of the classroom such as quickly creating a graph or problem solution to respond electronically to a question from a student. This interest in TabletPCs led to discussions within the college of a possible initiative to put TabletPCs into the hands of faculty. A memo to the faculty to determine their level of interest resulted in strong expressions of interest by nearly thirty faculty members, so the TabletPC initiative was started. A key element of the program was that the TabletPCs, which were purchased with a three-way split of funding from the home department, the college, and the university, would belong to the faculty member as long as they participated in workshops and assessment related to the project. Other important elements in the success were one-on-one support from an instructional specialist in the college and the participation of the computer support staff from the participating departments.

Assessment of the impact of this program is currently underway with support from the Leonhard Center. Faculty report enhanced ability to reuse and refine the digital instructional materials; efficient sharing of digital materials, including complete class notes, with their students; and more interaction with students during class. Students indicate that the use of the TabletPC increases their attention, engagement, and understanding (Toto, Wharton, Cimbala, and Wise, 2006). Another indication of the success of this approach is that other faculty members are asking about joining the program.

Lesson learned: The common characteristic that led to the success of the faculty-centered support provided in the ethics workshop and TabletPC initiative was that each met needs identified by a substantial number of faculty members. This is in contrast to some efforts that were pursued in an "if we build it, they will come" mode. For example, workshops on critical areas such as the use of technology in the classroom and the more effective use of collaborative learning have gone largely unattended because a critical mass of faculty members had not been involved in the identification of such workshops as vital to meeting their needs.

Conclusion

In this chapter, we have summarized some of our experiences in implementing major reforms at the college, department, and faculty levels. In carrying out each of these reforms, we have learned a great deal about the change process. We have sought here to share those aspects of the change process that we believe can be translated to other institutions like Penn State, and perhaps even those that are substantially different from it. In undertaking substantial reforms, the major points we have learned are:

- Create a supportive climate for change and innovation.
- Provide strong leadership at the college, department, and faculty levels.
- Include all parties in reaching decisions.
- Recognize the demands on faculty members.
- Provide necessary resources and appropriate incentives.
- Provide the support required to bring about change, which may include establishing a teaching and learning center.
- Assess the impact of the change.

References

Astin, A. W. "Engineering Outcomes." *ASEE Prism,* Sept. 1993, pp. 27–30.
Bransford, J. D., Brown, A. L., and Cocking, R. R. *How People Learn: Brain, Mind, Experience, and School.* Washington, D.C.: National Academy Press, 2000.
Clark, M. C., Froyd, J., Merton, P., and Richardson, J. "The Evolution of Curricular Change Models Within the Foundation Coalition." *Journal of Engineering Education,* 2004, *93*(1), 37–47.
Cross, K. P. "Leading Edge Efforts to Improve Teaching and Learning: The Hesburgh Awards." *Change,* 2001, *33*(4), 30–37.
Davis, M. *Ethics and the University.* London: Routledge Press, 1999.
Felder, R. M., Felder, G. N., and Dietz, E. J. "A Longitudinal Study of Engineering Student Performance and Retention. V. Comparisons with Traditionally-Taught Students." *Journal of Engineering Education,* 1998, *87*(4) 469–480.
Fromm, E. "The Changing Engineering Educational Paradigm." *Journal of Engineering Education,* 2003, *92*(2), 113–121.
Hewitt, N. M., and Seymour, E. "A Long, Discouraging Climb." *ASEE Prism,* Feb. 1992, pp. 24–28.
Litzinger, T., and others. "Learning and Teaching Ethics in Engineering: Preparing Engineering Faculty to Teach Ethics." In *Proceedings of the ASEE Annual Conference and Exposition.* Washington, D.C.: American Society for Engineering Education, 2003.
National Academy of Sciences, National Academy of Engineering, and Institute of Medicine. *Rising Above the Gathering Storm.* Washington, D.C.: National Academy Press, 2005.
National Science Board. *Science and Engineering Indicators 2006.* Arlington, Va.: National Science Foundation, 2006.
Olds, B. M., and Miller, R. L. "The Effect of a First-Year Integrated Engineering Curriculum on Graduation Rates and Student Satisfaction: A Longitudinal Study." *Journal of Engineering Education,* 2004, *93*(1) 23–35.

Seymour, E. "Tracking the Processes of Change in U.S. Undergraduate Education in Science, Mathematics, Engineering, and Technology." *Science Education,* 2002, *86*(1), 79–105.

Simpson, T. W., and others. "IME, Inc.: A New Course for Integrating Design, Manufacturing, and Production into the Engineering Curriculum." *International Journal of Engineering Education,* 2004, *20*(5), 764–776.

Singer, S. R. "Learning and Teaching Centers: Hubs of Educational Reform." In J. L. Narum and K. Conover (eds.), *Building Robust Learning Environments in Undergraduate Science, Technology, Engineering, and Mathematics.* New Directions for Higher Education, no. 119. San Francisco: Jossey-Bass, 2002.

Sunal, D. W., and others. "Teaching Science in Higher Education: Faculty Professional Development and Barriers to Change." *School Science and Mathematics,* 2001, *101*(5), 246–257.

Toto, R., Wharton, M., Cimbala, J., and Wise, J. "One Step Beyond: Lecturing With a TabletPC." In *Proceedings of the 2006 ASEE Annual Conference and Exposition.* Washington, D.C.: American Society for Engineering Education, 2006.

THOMAS A. LITZINGER is director of the Leonhard Center for the Enhancement of Engineering Education and a professor of mechanical engineering at Penn State University.

RICHARD J. KOUBEK is head of the Harold and Inge Marcus Department of Industrial and Manufacturing Engineering at Penn State University.

DAVID N. WORMLEY is Marcus Chair and dean of the college of engineering at Penn State University.

NEW DIRECTIONS FOR TEACHING AND LEARNING • DOI: 10.1002/tl

5

Initiatives designed to enhance STEM undergraduate education have much in common, as well as distinctive differences by field.

Discipline-Based Efforts to Enhance Undergraduate STEM Education

Joan Ferrini-Mundy, Beste Güçler

Efforts to reform and improve teaching and learning in the undergraduate science, technology, engineering, and mathematics (STEM) disciplines have grown increasingly stronger and more focused over the past two decades. Since the early 1990s, some notable unifying developments have given coherence to such initiatives, as well as other developments that have contributed to their disciplinary depth and embeddedness. Here we provide some historical perspective on the ways in which these reform efforts have evolved. National organizations and entities, including the National Research Council (NRC), National Science Foundation (NSF), Project Kaleidoscope (PKAL), accrediting agencies, and coalitions of institutions of higher education, as well as efforts in which disciplinary professional societies have been deeply involved, have had significant influence.

The 1986 report of the National Science Board (National Science Foundation, 1986), *Undergraduate Science, Mathematics, and Engineering Education,* known as the Neal Report, called for an NSF program to support improved education for undergraduate STEM students. Out of this grew

This material was based on work supported in part by the National Science Foundation while the first author was working at the foundation. We appreciate the ideas and information provided by Terry Woodin, National Science Foundation, in the preparation of this chapter. The assistance that was supplied by J. Reid Schewebach, National Science Foundation, and Jean Beland, Michigan State University, was invaluable as well. The views expressed here are those of the authors and are not necessarily those of the National Science Foundation.

NEW DIRECTIONS FOR TEACHING AND LEARNING, no. 117, Spring 2009 © Wiley Periodicals, Inc.
Published online in Wiley InterScience (www.interscience.wiley.com) • DOI: 10.1002/tl.344

NSF's Division for Undergraduate Education, which has the education of undergraduate students as its first priority.

Ten years later, NSF's Education and Human Resources Advisory Committee produced a report, *Shaping the Future: New Expectations for Undergraduate Education in Science, Mathematics, Engineering and Technology* (1996), which included recommendations to promote the improvement of undergraduate education in the STEM fields. These recommendations centered on holding high expectations and supporting students and providing excellent pedagogy. The goal was "that all students have access to supportive, excellent undergraduate education in science, mathematics, engineering, and technology, and all students learn these subjects by direct experience with the methods and processes of inquiry" (p. 1). The report also suggests that STEM departments should have a major responsibility for promoting high-quality undergraduate learning, setting standards, putting accountability systems in place, and engaging a broad spectrum of students.

A number of other organizations also have focused strongly on the improvement of undergraduate teaching and learning. These include Project Kaleidoscope (PKAL), founded in 1991, whose agenda is the reform of undergraduate STEM education. This agenda, with its rationale, is presented in *What Works—Building Natural Science Communities* (PKAL, 1991) and at the first PKAL National Colloquium at the National Academy of Sciences in 1991:

> Project Kaleidoscope (PKAL) focuses on building learning environments that attract and sustain undergraduate students to the study of STEM fields and motivate them to consider careers in related fields. PKAL works to equip teams of faculty and administrators for leadership in reform at the local level, so that students and science are better served, as well as to encourage broad understanding of how strong undergraduate STEM programs serve the national interest. [http://www.pkal.org/documents/About.cfm].

Throughout this same period, various professional organizations have assumed leadership roles in reform efforts. For instance, in the early 1990s, the Mathematical Association of America, with external funding from the Exxon Foundation, initiated Project NExT, "a professional development program for new or recent Ph.D.s in the mathematical sciences that addresses all aspects of an academic career, with an emphasis on the teaching and learning of mathematics" (Project NExT http://archives.math.utk.edu/projnext/). Part of the intention was to help beginning mathematics faculty make the transition from graduate training in research to teaching responsibilities in the classroom (MacKenzie, 1997).

Coalitions of institutions of higher education also have proved to be a force in focusing attention on undergraduate reform. The Engineering Education Coalitions program "currently includes eight consortia or 'coalitions' of engineering schools of diverse size and mission. Each coalition works to develop, implement, and evaluate forms of engineering education that reflect the new paradigm. The eight coalitions encompass more than fifty engineering schools, which annually confer more than one-third of the baccalaureate engineering degrees in the United States" (Prados, 1998, p. 3).

Many of these efforts for improvement in the teaching and learning of STEM at the undergraduate level have been driven by concerns about attracting people to STEM careers and retaining them in those careers, increasing diversity in the STEM fields, and ensuring the capacity for continued STEM advances by providing more current and forward-looking undergraduate experiences.

Strategies for the improvement of undergraduate STEM learning can be categorized into three types. Capacity-building strategies involve building networks and communities of individuals (for example, PKAL, Project NExT), all committed to improving teaching and learning at the undergraduate level. Such strategies also emphasize the need to fill the pipeline in given fields. Curricular strategies have been focused on improving the materials and resources available for the teaching of undergraduate students. These include introducing technology, rethinking traditional content, organizing courses around interdisciplinary ideas, providing authentic research experiences to undergraduates, and keeping material current and representative of new directions in the discipline. The strategies in the third group are pedagogical: improving the teaching of undergraduate STEM content by using such innovations as probes or clickers, small groups or peer-assisted instruction in large lectures, and instructional assessments such as diagnostic concept inventories and one-minute essays.

In the sections that follow, we provide examples of discipline-based efforts to improve and enhance STEM education drawn from the past two decades. These examples were chosen to emphasize the range of geneses, approaches, and impacts in undergraduate reform. In mathematics, calculus reform began as a curricular strategy and evolved to include pedagogical elements as well. Reform in the biological sciences has been quite focused on ensuring that majors in the biological disciplines have the opportunity to experience the discipline as it is taking shape at the frontiers of research, and thus has a focus on both curriculum and capacity building. In engineering, reform has been driven by interest in attracting and retaining engineers to the profession, and ensuring that prospective engineers have a meaningful educational experience, another area where capacity building has been a focus. And reform in physics education has grown from research about the teaching and learning of physics and has a strong curricular focus.

Mathematics: The Calculus Reform Movement

In the period from the mid-1980s through the early 1990s, the undergraduate mathematics community engaged in a concerted effort to overhaul the teaching and curriculum of beginning calculus. Concerns about college enrollment and retention rates and about the depth and breadth of students' understanding of college mathematics also drove these discussions (Douglas, 1986; National Science Foundation, 1986, 1989; Steen, 1987) and led to a conference held at Tulane University in 1986. The conference had two main themes: calculus courses should address fewer topics, and students should learn through active engagement with the material (Douglas, 1986). From this context, the calculus reform movement emerged.

The reform promoted fundamental changes in the curriculum and the pedagogy of beginning calculus, with emphasis on conceptual understanding rather than procedural skills, integration of the applications of calculus in the curriculum, and the use of computers to provide students with laboratory experience. Technology was incorporated with pedagogy, multiple representations of one concept were promoted, and the use of discovery, cooperative learning, and problem solving in undergraduate calculus classrooms was advocated (Ganter, 1999).

The improvement and growing availability of educational technology, which allowed the dynamic interpretations of central calculus topics such as functions and their graphs, was also a factor. Somewhat in contrast to the K–12 standards of the time (National Council of Teachers of Mathematics, 1989), which were based in part on theory and research about teaching and learning, the calculus reform was driven more by interest from the field in streamlining the content and improving student success. Mathematicians who were interested in teaching and curriculum were heavily involved and led many of the projects. NSF (1986, 1988) initiated a program to fund curriculum development, and 127 projects were supported at universities across the country over a six-year period (Ganter, 1999).

Ferrini-Mundy, Lauten, and Graham (1998) undertook a formative evaluation of the Calculus Consortium based at Harvard (CCH), one of the NSF-supported projects. Their survey findings indicated that students who were taking the CCH courses believed symbolic manipulations, graphical methods, and numerical tables were useful for understanding calculus. They had positive attitudes toward the multiple assessment techniques and thought that being able to write about calculus was a good way of assessing their knowledge. However, when asked to assign points to some specific aspects of the reform calculus classes, respondents assigned the higher scores to lectures in comparison to discussion classes and to homework compared to group work and individual projects. Thus, it may be that not all aspects of the reforms were well received by students. It would be interesting to reexamine this area to gauge whether K–12 mathematics education reform may have influenced the attitudes of college students.

Ganter's analysis (1999) of the 127 NSF-funded projects to support calculus reform efforts indicates that it is difficult to claim the reform took hold. Especially in the beginning years of the implementations, faculty and students reported negative attitudes toward the curricular and pedagogical aspects of the reform. Ganter indicates that even the faculty members who were interested in adopting the reform practices had difficulty adjusting to new ways of teaching that required expertise in using technology, knowing a variety of applications, or implementing a student-centered approach. The calculus reform was not uniformly well received, and generated considerable controversy within the mathematics community. Hughes Hallett (2000), one of the leaders of the Harvard Calculus project, notes that in spite of the controversies, many aspects of the calculus reform—the emphasis on conceptual understanding and multiple representations, together with increased use of technology since the early 1990s—are so embedded in calculus practice that they are considered mainstream.

Research about the effectiveness of calculus reform has not been systematic; many reports are in the form of unpublished doctoral dissertations (Ganter, 1999). Mostly they are studies that compare control (traditional) calculus courses and experimental reform calculus courses (see Armstrong, 1994; Garner and Garner, 2001; Maher, 2000; Roddick, 1995; Stick, 1997). Multiple reform approaches have been implemented in universities, so aggregation of findings is not necessarily appropriate.

Hughes Hallett (2000) mentions that the calculus reform has increased the opportunity for cooperation between mathematics and other fields and suggests that efforts to make calculus courses more responsive to the needs of other disciplines led to the Mathematical Association of America's Curriculum Foundations Project (http://www.maa.org/cupm/crafty/cf_project.html). This effort produced a report based on workshops with faculty from outside mathematics (Ganter and Barker, 2004). Faculty from such diverse areas as biology, business, chemistry, computer science, several areas of engineering, and the life sciences met with mathematicians to discuss the mathematical preparation needs of majors. One workshop focused on the preparation of mathematics majors. The report from that group argues for the need to "move students from a procedural/computational understanding of mathematics to a broad understanding encompassing logical reasoning, generalization, abstraction, and formal proof" (Kasube and McCallum, 2004, p. 109). Some elements of calculus reform may have influenced this initiative.

The Biological Sciences: Reform of the Teaching of Biology

Drivers for reform in the biological sciences have been the combination of major changes in the discipline together with major changes in what is known from research about teaching and learning, as well as educational technologies. Educational reform at the undergraduate level in biology currently includes emphasis on the role of computation in biology.

Two major reports have had a crucial role in promoting reform of biology teaching and learning at the undergraduate level: the Howard Hughes Medical Institute (HHMI) *Beyond Bio 101: The Transformation of Undergraduate Biology Education* (Howard Hughes Medical Institute, 1996) and *BIO*

2010: Transforming Undergraduate Education for Future Research Biologists issued by the Board on Life Science of the National Research Council in 2003.

Beyond Bio 101 is based on the experiences of many of the 220 colleges and universities that have been awarded more than $335 million in grants since 1988 from HHMI's Undergraduate Biological Sciences Education Program to undertake reform. Some key features of the initiatives undertaken in biology resonate with some of what occurred in the calculus reform initiative. The report indicates emphasis on active learning, use of technology, and curricular revisions aimed at more effective teaching of particular topics. In particular, the use of information technologies has been prominent in biological reforms, including the use of digital photographs from laboratory demonstrations, as well as communications innovations to put students and faculty in more constant contact, such as e-mail, chatrooms, and bulletin board innovations. Other components of the reform included innovations in infrastructure to promote involvement of faculty, such as minigrant programs and curricular innovations engaging faculty and their entry-level students in discussions about the faculty members' research. In the sciences in general, and the biological sciences in particular, providing students with undergraduate hands-on and undergraduate literature-based research opportunities also has been a priority in order to engage students as working scientists (Lopatto, 2004).

BIO 2010: Transforming Undergraduate Education for Future Research Biologists makes the claim that there has been relatively minimal change in undergraduate biology education in two decades, and "the ways in which most future biologists are educated are geared to the biology of the past, rather than the biology of the present or the future" (National Research Council, 2003, p. 1). The report advocates teaching biology not as a collection of facts but rather through emphasis on the history of the field and the nature of scientific discovery. There is a focus on interdisciplinarity and integration of ideas, on the basis of changes in the nature of biology and how biological research is performed, and in particular on the importance of preparation in the physical, mathematical, and information sciences. The importance of interdisciplinary laboratory courses and student research experiences is also underscored.

Several studies have examined the outcomes of undergraduate research experiences (see Boylan, 1997), and although the studies include fields other than the biological sciences, the results are relevant. They indicate that those who have had undergraduate research experiences report generally greater interest in science and engineering research, deeper understanding of the scientific research process, and a wider sense of the career possibilities in these fields.

Engineering Education Reform

Engineering education has experienced major paradigm changes over the past fifty years (Prados, 1998), moving from a highly practical subject in the pre–World War II era to a more academic subject, drawing on mathematics and engineering science and producing research. Today developments in information technology and globalization require engineers not only to have technical expertise but also to know how engineering is tied to other disciplines and the industrial market. Many argue that engineering graduates are inadequately prepared to meet the demands of the domain in knowledge of global issues, expertise in human dimensions of technology and effective communication, and teamwork skills (Todd, Sorensen, and Magleby, 1993; McMasters and Lang, 1995; Wulf and Fisher, 2002; Splitt, 2003). Moreover, fewer students enroll in engineering programs, and the dropout rates are alarmingly high (Wulf and Fisher, 2002). A series of reports raised issues about diversity, preparation, recruitment, and retention (see National Academy of Engineering, 2004, National Academy of Sciences, 2005; National Research Council, 1989; Board on Engineering Education, 1995). Concerns about the state of the engineering workforce are discussed in detail in the National Research Council's *Rising Above the Gathering Storm* (2005).

Both pedagogical and curricular revisions in engineering education have been advocated. Private foundations, industry advisory boards of engineering departments, and the Accreditation Board for Engineering and Technology (ABET) also have been instrumental in the reforms in this discipline. These organizations supported the new direction of engineering education with funds, investment in further research, and support for the new aspects of engineering education such as team-based collaborative learning.

Prados (1998) argued that the reform would involve changing passive, lecture-based instruction approaches to active and project-based learning. The integration of subject matter from other disciplines, scientific and mathematical concepts with their applications information technology, and connections with industry would also be promoted. Besides these curricular changes, Wulf and Fisher (2002) identified five more areas that needed reform: the current faculty reward structure that values research over teaching, acceptance of the baccalaureate as a professional engineering degree, formalizing lifelong learning to keep engineers up to date with the demands of the field and industry, enhancing diversity in engineering programs, and improving technological literacy in the general population.

A new set of standards for engineering education was adopted by ABET in 1996. *Engineering Criteria 2000* (EC2000) shifted the basis for accreditation to "what is learned rather than what is taught." Wulf and Fisher (2002) note that ABET's adoption of EC2000 enabled the development of outcome-oriented programs that can structure their own curriculum according to the specific needs of their students. EC200 emphasized problem solving and communication skills, societal and global issues, and ethics. Lattuca, Terenzini, and Volkwein (2006) studied the impact of EC2000 and found many changes in engineering programs following EC2000, including greater emphasis on skills needed for the profession and learning in active modes within engineering curricula. They also report that 2004 engineering graduates claimed to be more actively engaged in their own learning, interacting more with instructors. An assessment of learning outcomes found "2004 graduates better prepared than their 1994 counterparts" (p. 7) and evidence of gains in professional skills and maintenance of technical skills.

Despite these steps to improve engineering education, Splitt (2003) argues that there seems to be no clear path forward and progress is slow due to academic resistance to change. He underlines that scholarly aspects of engineering have no immediate financial and academic rewards, and promotion is still based heavily on research. Indeed, Lattuca, Terenzini, and Volkwein (2006) found in their survey that although there were high levels of faculty support for continuous improvement, there was still only a mixed emphasis on teaching in the faculty reward structure. Moreover, the ABET criteria suggested create the perception of an imposed solution, which is considered "too ideal" to implement under the current real-world circumstances (Splitt, 2003). It seems that although the direction of change is clear, engineering struggles with how to put it into action.

The Physical Sciences: Improving the Teaching and Learning of Physics

Reform in undergraduate physics education seems to have roots in part in the field of physics education research. A field that goes back to the early 1980s (see McDermott, 1984; Reif, 1986; Trowbridge and McDermott, 1980), physics education research has sought to document student misconceptions and understand students' understanding of specific concepts. On the basis of this work, and sometimes in concert with it, scholars have developed a variety of activity-based curricular materials (see Laws, 2004). Laws acknowledges that the approach is "based in large part on the guided inquiry materials pioneered by McDermott et al. (1996) at the University of Washington" (p. 247). The development of the Force Concept Inventory (Halloun and Hestenes, 1985a, 1985b), a test of conceptual understanding of Newtonian mechanics, was instrumental in engaging the physics community in conversations about students' conceptual understanding.

According to Hilborn, Howes, and Krane (2003), *Shaping the Future* (NSF, 1996, 1998) also presented an important catalyst to the physics community. It challenged undergraduate physics educators to consider whether undergraduate physics programs are accessible to and effective for all students and whether they provide students with direct experience with the methods and processes of inquiry. In response a group of undergraduate physics, mathematics, engineering, and chemistry educators joined together under the direction of the American Association of Physics Teachers to consider the current state of undergraduate physics and recommend future directions for the physics community. The result of their efforts, *Physics at the Crossroads* (American Association of Physics Teachers, 1996), summarized findings from various sources and urged the physics education community to take recommendations for change very seriously and develop methods and infrastructure for supporting undergraduate physics education reform.

A characteristic of physics education reform, perhaps having some commonality with calculus reform, was the notion that physics education needed to reach more than those students who would go on to become physicists. Rather, the reform had some commitment to creating physics learning experiences that would serve students interested in a wider range of science and technology areas.

According to the authors of *Physics at the Crossroads*, a confluence of events made it possible to pursue an agenda of physics education reform. Evidence from research was supporting the use of active learning and pedagogies that featured strong student engagement. An outgrowth of the physics education research movement was the production of new instructional materials and resources based on findings about student learning. In 1999 the National Task Force on Undergraduate Physics (http://www.aapt.org/Projects/ntfup.cfm) was established as a joint effort of the three physics professional organizations. A product of this effort was the *Strategic Programs for Innovations in Undergraduate Physics* (SPIN-UP) report (Hilborn, Howes, and Krane, 2003), which launched a program of visits to twenty-one physics departments whose undergraduate programs were seen as successful. Their findings indicated that departmental commitment and responsibility, mentoring, undergraduate research opportunities, departmental leadership, and disposition toward continual improvement and evaluation all were visible in these departments.

Common Themes and Notable Differences

It is not surprising that the discipline-based efforts to improve undergraduate STEM teaching and learning, although sharing some common features, also vary in interesting ways. Here we highlight both commonalities and distinctions.

Among factors that are common in all the reform approaches are the emphases on the use of technology and applications. It seems clear that all the fields try to incorporate technological advances into undergraduate curriculum in order to provide their students current tools for working on authentic problems. Although the focus of engineering, biology, and, possibly, physics on applications may result from the nature of the fields, the focus of the mathematics community on the same issue points to another common element that lies behind the reform initiatives: interdisciplinary collaboration. This goal is most visible for engineering and physics reforms, where there are deliberate efforts to offer interdisciplinary courses and programs. In that sense, all reform approaches summarized here attempt to

NEW DIRECTIONS FOR TEACHING AND LEARNING • DOI: 10.1002/tl

broaden the local knowledge of the specific fields with the integration of knowledge and applications of the other fields.

In all of these areas—mathematics, biology, engineering, and physics—the motivations and energy for making improvements were generated in large measure from within the disciplinary fields themselves. However, in all cases, in order for reforms to go forward, other kinds of outside influences were important, ranging from accrediting organizations, to the needs of related disciplines, to the support of funding agencies. In mathematics, concerns about high failure rates in introductory calculus raised worries for the mathematics field that it would be difficult to keep students interested and engaged in mathematical study. This is similar to the apparent motivations for physics education reform, which included concerns from the physics community that students were not coming to understand the difficult concepts of introductory physics, and thereby limiting their future involvement.

In the biological sciences, it seemed that reform efforts have been driven in part by changes in the discipline itself and by the view that the training of current biology students should reflect more fully the nature of the discipline, particularly with an emphasis on interdisciplinary connections. Engineering reform addresses similar problems since it is based on concerns about attrition and retention rates as well as the inadequate preparation of engineers for the requirements of the field.

Thus in all cases, these reforms do seem to be about increasing access and success in terms of students' understanding. The emphases within the reforms in terms of pedagogy seem to show similar characteristics. All advocate versions of active, project-based, and collaborative learning strategies compared to more traditional teaching approaches. Moreover, all encourage problem solving and communication skills. Mathematics and physics reform approaches explicitly include conceptual understanding as one of their primary goals.

The emphases within the reforms, in terms of curriculum, varied. Although the Tulane conference on calculus reform was focused on the notion of a "lean and lively calculus" with a streamlined list of topics, when the Calculus Consortium at Harvard's materials failed to include the intermediate value theorem, there was an uproar from parts of the mathematics community. So the primary impact of the overall calculus reform effort may have been more pedagogical, through the introduction of more technology into the instruction of calculus, a stronger focus on visual representation, and emphasis on applied problems.

In contrast, in both engineering and biology, it seems that the reforms are characterized by a strong emphasis on trying to acquaint students with the experience and work of researchers in the discipline and in making changes in curriculum to reflect future trends and directions in the fields.

NEW DIRECTIONS FOR TEACHING AND LEARNING • DOI: 10.1002/tl

Conclusion

At this time of significant focus on both U.S. global competitiveness and improved scientific literacy for all, the pressure to sustain high-quality undergraduate teaching and learning experiences in the STEM disciplines is perhaps unprecedented. The brief accounts provided here of efforts in multiple disciplines to heighten attention to quality teaching and learning indicate a national will and commitment in colleges and universities across the nation to hypothesize, invent, design, implement, and test innovative means of ensuring that students learn the STEM disciplines to the levels needed for competitiveness and for literacy. The challenges are also significant in introducing new approaches and studying their impact. The process of reforming undergraduate STEM learning is ongoing, and the combined engagement of disciplinary researchers and teachers, together with experts in STEM teaching and learning, buoyed by professional societies and funders, seems the right combination to ensure that changes and refinements will become an ongoing component of undergraduate STEM education.

References

American Association of Physics Teachers. *Physics at the Crossroads.* College Park, Md.: American Association of Physics Teachers, 1996.

Armstrong, G. "Our Experience with Two Reformed Calculus Programs." *Primus,* 1994, 4(4), 301–311.

Board on Engineering Education. *Engineering Education: Designing an Adaptive System.* Washington, D.C.: National Academy Press, 1995.

Boylan, M. G. "Non-vanishing of the Partition Function Modulo Small Primes." 2006. Retrieved Jan. 20, 2009, from http://www.math.sc.edu/~boylan/reprints/modthree.3.pdf.

Douglas, R. G. (ed.). *Toward a Lean and Lively Calculus.* Washington, D.C.: Mathematical Association of America, 1986.

Engineering Accreditation Commission. *Engineering Criteria 2000.* (2nd ed.) Baltimore, Md.: Accreditation Board for Engineering and Technology, 1997.

Ferrini-Mundy, J., Lauten, D., and Graham, K. *Calculus Consortium Based at Harvard Evaluation and Documentation Project Report.* Durham: University of New Hampshire, 1998.

Ganter, S. L. "An Evaluation of Calculus Reform: A Preliminary Report of a National Study." In B. Gold, S. Keith, and W. Marion (eds.), *Assessment Practices in Undergraduate Mathematics.* Washington, D.C.: Mathematical Association of America, 1999.

Ganter, S. L., and Barker, W. (eds.). *Curriculum Foundations Project: Voices of the Partner Disciplines.* Washington, D.C.: Mathematical Association of America, 2004.

Garner, B. E., and Garner, L. E. "Retention of Concepts and Skills in Traditional and Reformed Applied Calculus." *Mathematics Education Research Journal,* 2001, 13(3), 165–184.

Halloun, I., and Hestenes, D. "Common Sense Concepts About Motion." *American Journal of Physics,* 1985a, 53, 1056–1065.

Halloun, I., and Hestenes, D. "The Initial Knowledge State of College Physics Students." *American Journal of Physics,* 1985b, 53, 1043–1055.

Hilborn, R. C., Howes, R. H., and Krane, K. S. *Strategic Programs for Innovations in Undergraduate Physics: Project report.* College Park, Md.: American Association of Physics Teachers, 2003.

Howard Hughes Medical Institute. *Beyond Bio 101: The Transformation of Undergradu-
ate Biology Education.* Chevy Chase, Md.: Howard Hughes Medical Institute, 1996.
Hughes Hallett, D. "Calculus at the Start of the New Millennium." In *Proceedings of the
International Conference on Technology in Mathematics Education.* Beirut, Lebanon:
Lebanese American University, 2000.
Kasube, H., and McCallum, W. "Mathematics." In S. Ganter and W. Barker (eds.), *The
Curriculum Foundations Project: Voices of the Partner Disciplines.* Washington, D.C.:
Mathematical Association of America, 2004.
Lattuca, L., Terenzini, P., and Volkwein, J. F. *Engineering Change: A Study of the Impact
of EC2000.* University Park: Center for the Study of Higher Education, Pennsylvania
State University, 2006.
Laws, P. W. "Promoting the Diffusion of Undergraduate Science Curriculum Reform:
The Activity-Based Physics Suite as an Example." In American Association for the
Advancement of Science (ed.), *Invention and Impact: Building Excellence in Undergrad-
uate Science, Technology, Engineering and Mathematics Education.* Washington, D.C.:
American Association for the Advancement of Science, 2004.
Lopatto, D. "What Undergraduate Research Can Tell Us About Research on Learning."
Washington, D.C.: Project Kaleidoscope, 2004.
MacKenzie, D. "Mathematics Teaching: Project NExT Helps New Ph.D.s in the
Classroom—And Beyond." *Science,* 1997, 277(5329), 1031–1032.
Maher, R. J. "Reform in the First Year Calculus Sequence for Mathematics and Science
Majors: An Eleven Year Study." *Primus,* 2000, *10*(3), 267–272.
McDermott, L. C. "Research on Conceptual Understanding in Mechanics." *Physics
Today,* 1984, *61,* 295–298.
McMasters, J. H., and Lang, J. D. "Enhancing Engineering and Manufacturing Educa-
tion: Industry Needs, Industry Roles." Paper presented at the American Society for
Engineering Education Annual Conference and Exposition, Anaheim, Calif., 1995.
National Academy of Engineering. *The Engineer of 2020: Vision of Engineering in the New
Century.* Washington, D.C.: National Academy Press, 2004.
National Academy of Sciences, National Academy of Engineering, and Institute of Med-
icine. *Rising Above the Gathering Storm: Energizing and Employing America for a
Brighter Economic Future.* Washington, D.C.: National Research Council, 2005.
National Council of Teachers of Mathematics. *Curriculum and Evaluation Standards for
School Mathematics—Executive Summary.* Reston, Va.: National Council of Teachers
of Mathematics, 1989.
National Research Council. *Everybody Counts: A Report to the Nation on the Future of
Mathematics Education.* Washington, D.C.: National Research Council and Mathemat-
ical Sciences Education Board, 1989.
National Research Council. *BIO 2010: Transforming Undergraduate Education for Future
Research Biologists.* Washington, D.C.: National Research Council, 2003.
National Science Foundation. *Undergraduate Science, Mathematics and Engineering Educa-
tion: Role for the National Science Foundation and Recommendations for Action by Other Sec-
tors to Strengthen Collegiate Education and Pursue Excellence in the Next Generation of U.S.
Leadership in Science and Technology.* Washington, D.C.: National Science Board, 1986.
National Science Foundation. *Report on the National Science Foundation Disciplinary
Workshops on Undergraduate Education: Recommendations of the Disciplinary Taskforces
Concerning Critical Issues in U.S. Undergraduate Education in the Sciences, Mathemat-
ics and Engineering, Division of Undergraduate Science, Engineering, and Mathematics
Education.* Washington, D.C.: Directorate for Science and Engineering Education,
National Science Foundation, 1989.
National Science Foundation. *Shaping the Future: New Expectations for Undergraduate
Education in Science, Mathematics, Engineering, and Technology.* Arlington, Va.:
National Science Foundation, 1996.

National Science Foundation. *Shaping the Future. Vol. 2: Perspectives on Education in Science, Mathematics, Engineering, and Technology.* Arlington, Va.: National Science Foundation, 1998.

Prados, J. W. "Engineering Education in the United States: Past, Present and Future." 1998. Retrieved Feb. 12, 2008, from http://www.ineer.org/Events/ICEE1998/Icee/papers/255.pdf.

Project Kaleidoscope (PKAL). *What Works: Building Natural Science Communities, A Plan for Strengthening Undergraduate Science and Mathematics (Vol. 1).* Washington, D.C.: Project Kaleidoscope, 1991.

Project NExT: A Program of the Mathematical Association of America. Retrieved Jan. 18, 2009, from http://archives.math.utk.edu/projnext/.

Reif, F. "Scientific Approaches to Science Education." *Physics Today,* 1986, *39*(11), 48–54.

Roddick, C. S. "How Students Use Their Knowledge of Calculus in an Engineering Mechanics Course." Paper presented at the Annual Meeting of the North American Chapter of the International Group for the Psychology of Mathematics Education. Columbus, Ohio, Oct. 21–24, 1995.

Splitt, F. J. "Engineering Education Reform: A Trilogy." Paper presented at the Annual Meeting of The International Engineering Consortium. Chicago: Oct. 2003.

Steen, L. A. (ed.). *Calculus for a New Century: A Pump, Not a Filter.* Washington, D.C.: Mathematical Association of America, 1987.

Stick, M. E. "Calculus Reform and Graphing Calculators: A University View." *Mathematics Teacher,* 1997, *90*(5), 356–360, 363.

Todd, R. H., Sorensen, C. D., and Magleby S. P. "Designing a Capstone Senior Course to Satisfy Industrial Customers." *Journal of Engineering Education,* 1993, *82*(2), 92–100.

Trowbridge, D. E., and McDermott, L. C. "Investigation of Student Understanding of the Concept of Velocity in One Dimension." *American Journal of Physics,* 1980, *48*, 1020–1028.

Wulf, W. A., and Fisher, G.M.C. "A Makeover for Engineering Education." *Issues in Science and Technology,* 2002, *18*(3), 35–39.

JOAN FERRINI-MUNDY is a University Distinguished Professor of mathematics education at Michigan State University and division director of the National Science Foundation's Division of Research on Learning and Informal Settings, in the Directorate for Education and Human Resources.

BESTE GÜÇLER is a doctoral student in the Division of Science and Mathematics Education at Michigan State University.

NEW DIRECTIONS FOR TEACHING AND LEARNING • DOI: 10.1002/tl

6

*This chapter considers how best to integrate STEM
education into the larger context of the undergraduate
experience to address important national concerns.*

The National Perspective: Fostering
the Enhancement of STEM
Undergraduate Education

Judith A. Ramaley

The investments of federal agencies in science, technology, engineering, and
mathematics (STEM) education are aimed at a single core question: How
can we ensure that the United States will have a well-prepared and innovative science and technology workforce in an era of increasing global competition? As the exploration of what this entails has progressed in recent
years, the purview has broadened to a larger topic: identifying and developing twenty-first-century skills by focusing on how the nature of work and
the economy are changing and an exploration of what it takes to be competitive in the new economy.

Within STEM education in particular, another critical component of
the larger context for examining the curriculum and the student experience
is the remarkable change in how science and engineering knowledge is
advanced today. This extraordinary revolution in the conduct of science and
engineering—the kinds of questions that can be asked, the technologies
available to address those questions, and the nature and complexity of the
scientific community itself—is leaving the typical undergraduate experience
further and further behind. It is no longer only a matter of attracting more
people to the study of science and engineering disciplines and making the
undergraduate experience more meaningful, as complex as those tasks are.
We now must also overhaul the curriculum and our approach to the student
experience in order to reflect the realities of how scientific understanding is

NEW DIRECTIONS FOR TEACHING AND LEARNING, no. 117, Spring 2009 © Wiley Periodicals, Inc.
Published online in Wiley InterScience (www.interscience.wiley.com) • DOI: 10.1002/tl.345

advanced today and how science and technology are shaping our society and our interactions with the rest of the world.

Why Is STEM Education Becoming a National Concern Today?

In the past five years, a number of reports have been prepared that offer a thoughtful exploration of the intersection of changes in the knowledge-based economy, new concepts of twenty-first-century skills for the workplace, and a consideration of the condition and capacities of our educational institutions. The following sketch of the context for rethinking STEM education is drawn from a summary of twenty-five of these reports recently prepared for the Innovation America Task Force commissioned by the National Governors Association, *Innovation America* (2006), and from the National Science Foundation Strategic Plan 2006–2011, entitled *Investing in America's Future* (2006), as well as from the fiscal year 2008 Administration Research and Development Budget Priorities prepared by the Office of Science and Technology Policy and Office of Management and Budget (2006). Each of these documents stands as a proxy for the broader national context that shapes discussions about STEM education.

The growth of the U.S. economy will be driven in large part by our nation's ability to generate ideas and translate them into competitive innovations and by the presence of a well-educated workforce that can implement those ideas. We will have a need "to ensure a scientifically literate population and a supply of qualified technical personnel commensurate with national need" who are prepared in such a way that they can work in an environment shaped by the rapid changes in how scientific knowledge is being advanced and how innovation is taking place (Marburger and Portman, 2006, p. 2). We must, however, prepare this workforce in new ways. According to the National Science Foundation Strategic Plan (2006), the conduct of science and engineering is changing rapidly, driven in part by the threefold increase in computing speed made possible by networked cyberinfrastructure and shaped by new technologies that provide a variety of sophisticated remote sensing capacities and observations of unprecedented detail and quality. As the plan explains, "Today's science . . . involves massive, accessible databases, digital libraries (many including sophisticated learning objects and materials), unique visualization environments and complex computational models" (National Science Foundation, 2006, p. 2).

As this remarkable advance in instrumentation and modeling capability has progressed, we can now distinguish between the simplified world represented in most instructional strategies and our new ability to explore much more closely the complexity of the real world. The world usually experienced by students is "discrete, static, sequential, mechanistic, separable, universal, homogeneous, regular, linear, surface, and single" and is based on simple models and diagrams. At the same time, the world revealed by advances in computation and sophisticated modeling is "continuous, dynamic, simultaneous, organic, interactive, conditional, heterogeneous, irregular, nonlinear, deep, and multiple" (Feltovich, Coulson, and Spiro, 2001). Few institutions other than research universities are likely to have a critical mass of STEM faculty who are themselves working in this mode. Fortunately, as the National Science Digital Library continues to expand its holdings, more and more faculty will be able to draw on simulations of this vast storehouse of complexity to bring the experience of their students closer to the reality of how science advances today.

We appear to be entering a new long cycle of economic change that will affect many of us. According to the original analysis by Joseph Strumpeter (cited by Robert Atkinson, 2004, pp. 3–4), "Economic history is best understood as a set of fundamental transformations from one kind of economy to another" during which the dominant forms of production stagnate, innovation wanes, and a new production system emerges that, after some hesitations, leads to "a new period of robust growth and innovation." These cycles are hypothesized to follow each other at about fifty-year intervals. Each wave places new demands on the educational system to create workers and citizens who can function in the environment being created by new technologies. Today we appear to be embarking on yet another wave, this time based on new forms of knowledge production and a revolution in information technology. Foray (2004, pp. ix–x) characterizes this new wave: "The rapid creation of new knowledge and the improvement of access to the knowledge bases thus constituted, in every possible way (education, training, transfer of technological knowledge, diffusion of innovations) are factors increasing economic efficiency, innovation, the quality of goods and services, and equity between individuals, social categories, and generations."

One of the consequences of these trends is that context matters less than it once did. Intellectual work can be transmitted electronically to any place where knowledge workers reside. At the same time, local educational systems and investments in human capital can influence where this knowledge work is done. In this knowledge-based economy, science and technology have become central drivers for the upward growth of the economy as a whole. The capacity to compete economically will rest increasingly on the extent to which a region or a nation has invested in education and in the research enterprise and can draw on workers with the needed skills. It is important to realize, however, that the production of high-end jobs is not confined to the knowledge-intensive parts of our economy. The implications of the knowledge age for how work is done throughout society and how we should educate for that work and for life are significant.

As we look forward into this century, there are many challenges ahead. Social stratification in this country has become increasingly linked to the system of education, especially postsecondary education. Whether a person enrolls in postsecondary education, the type of school he or she attends, and the amount of education he or she receives will have a profound effect on

NEW DIRECTIONS FOR TEACHING AND LEARNING • DOI: 10.1002/tl

occupational status, access to further career advancement, and quality of life (Commission on Work, Family and Citizenship, 1998). According to *The Forgotten Half Revisited: American Youth and Young Families, 1998–2008,* "In 1996 almost half of all adults (48.2 percent) either did not complete high school or terminated their formal education after graduation" (p. i). This may change since the report also reports a somewhat hopeful trend toward rising educational aspirations and attainment among late adolescents and young adults (ages eighteen to twenty-four). Unfortunately, only a third of young people from lower-income families go to college, while 83.4 percent of children from upper-income families do. These patterns have important implications for how we should approach our rethinking of education. We must rethink yet again what learning means, who our students are, how to close the gap in participation and educational achievement among various sectors of our society, and how to support the continuous learning that modern society and the new economy demand.

An Approach to Undergraduate STEM Education in a New Era

The frontiers of science and technology and the demands of an age of innovation are transcending traditional academic disciplines, surging past the structure and priorities of the typical academic department and drawing increasingly from many disciplines, including the arts and humanities and the social and behavioral sciences. To what extent have these emerging areas of science been introduced into the undergraduate curriculum, and how well are traditional departments managing to reflect in their own scholarly agendas and in their approach to STEM education the realities of how science and engineering are practiced today? Unfortunately, the answers are, respectively, "not often" and "not much." In recent years, there have been some wonderful experiments in redesigning the curriculum, the undergraduate laboratory experience, and even the overall student experience, but like all other such experiments, we still have a lot to learn about how to expand these efforts, take them to scale, and sustain and adapt them over time. We also have to learn how to document the impact of these experiments and satisfy with indisputable evidence the skepticism of colleagues who fail to see the need for change.

An especially good examination of this challenge is the *BIO 2010* report issued by the National Research Council in 2003. The findings are of substantive interest to scientists in all fields both because the changes in the several disciplines are similar and because of the growing intersection of disciplines. In addition, the external constraints to reform should sound familiar.

The premise of the National Research Council study on the biological sciences curriculum is that the undergraduate experience in biology is lagging seriously behind "how biologists design, perform and analyze experiments" (p. 1). The study represents our best exploration to date of just how much the nature of scientific investigation is changing and how little this remarkable shift is reflected in what undergraduates learn and how they learn. Although the primary focus of *BIO 2010* is on how to prepare the next generation of biomedical scientists, the issues themselves are relevant to a much broader audience. What should all of our students know about science? Can we find ways for them to learn science the way researchers do? Would students who learn science by doing science be more attracted to the field or better educated or both? The *BIO 2010* report is as much about the integration of the disciplines and about how research is done as it is about biology itself. As *BIO 2010* puts it, "The main idea of inquiry is for students to learn in the same way scientists learn through research." This is a goal that we can pursue in any field, and it is a worthy goal indeed.

Setting Different Expectations for Undergraduate Education

Our approach to STEM education can benefit from a larger view of how best to educate for the twenty-first century. Whether we are focusing on preparing the next generation of researchers and scholars or exploring how to educate a scientifically literate workforce and citizenry, we need to consider how our conversation fits into the larger question of our expectations of a college graduate. In 2002, the Greater Expectations panel issued a report calling for a fresh approach to liberal education that would produce graduates prepared for life and work who are "*intentional* about the process of acquiring learning, *empowered* by the mastery of intellectual and practical skills, *informed* by knowledge from various disciplines and *responsible* for their actions and those of society" (Leskes, 2004, p. iv). To accomplish this, an education must create an environment in which students can bring together their formal studies and their life experiences, explore and understand the worldviews of different fields, learn how to examine a complex issue from multiple perspectives, and bridge the often daunting gaps between theory and practice, contemplation and action. They also must experience directly how knowledge is generated and validated in an increasingly complex world. To address these issues, we must think past the borders of disciplines and academic departments.

As the Association of American Colleges and Universities and the Carnegie Foundation for the Advancement of Teaching have expressed it in their joint statement on Integrative Learning (Huber and Hutchings, 2004, p. 13), "Integrative learning comes in many varieties: connecting skills and knowledge from multiple sources and experiences; applying theory to practice in various settings utilizing diverse and even contradictory points of view; and, understanding issues and positions contextually."

At its best, the undergraduate STEM experience can become a working prototype of what all students should experience as intentional, empowered, informed, and responsible people ready to lead productive, responsible, and creative lives. In reality, however, many programs are built on a set of courses in which some integration is attempted within each individual course or seminar, but like the larger curriculum of which a STEM course sequence or major is a part, there is often very little intentional alignment or connection from one course to another. Rarely, if ever, do our students experience the kinds of learning and exploration that are characteristic of the new economy.

The major challenge facing contemporary higher education is to enhance its relevance and connectedness to the issues and problems faced by the broader society as these problems are defined by community members and not by academics acting independent of the views of others. To operate in this mode, previously defined boundaries that delineate disciplines, colleges, institutions, and communities must be opened up to accommodate shared goals, a shared agenda and mutual benefits, agreed-on definitions of success that are meaningful to both the university and community participants, and the pooling and leveraging of resources. This will change how the curriculum is designed and where the material comes from that we use as the starting point for learning and the consequences of learning itself.

Setting the Reform of STEM Undergraduate Education in Context

Any new approach to undergraduate reform must incorporate a number of core principles, all of which must be embraced and supported by the university community as a whole, not just by the STEM faculty. Our current approach, which often concentrates on improving a particular course or laboratory or a sequence of courses, will support only incremental change. What is needed now is a much broader, more encompassing approach to integrating STEM education into the larger context of the undergraduate experience. Unless an institution has a clear educational philosophy and a culture of shared expectations that pave the way for shared faculty responsibility for creating the conditions that allow that philosophy to be realized, our approaches to STEM education will of necessity have limited effects. Essentially, any reform of STEM undergraduate education must acknowledge and accommodate the distinctive setting in which the reform will be implemented. Without acknowledging contextual realities (such as institutional mission and philosophy, curriculum structure, instructional resources, learner attributes), the most well-intentioned education reform may be short-lived or not achieve its full potential.

- *Major curricular reform must be grounded in a clear institutional mission and a coherent educational philosophy that together create a framework and aspirations to guide the curricular reform process.* Peter Ewell wrote many years ago (a reference long since lost) that any curricular reform must be guided by an overall vision of learning itself, established through systematic research and the wisdom of practice (both hallmarks of an "expert culture"). Most reform efforts tend to be particularistic and mechanical. They result in add-ons rather than rethinking from within. The curriculum must be designed with a knowledge of how people learn and focused on those circumstances and strategies that promote learning.

The learner is not just a passive receptacle of knowledge but rather creates his or her own learning actively and uniquely by establishing and reworking patterns, relationships, and connections. We often forget that everyone learns all the time, both with us and without us, and that these forms of direct experience decisively shape individual understanding. Over the past few years, the work of the learning sciences makes clear that learning occurs best in the context of a compelling and interesting problem, it requires time and opportunity for reflection, and it occurs in a cultural context that provides both enjoyable interaction and personal support for all learners, as well as a chance to experience collaborative learning and teamwork.

In sum, any approach to significant rethinking of STEM education cannot be piecemeal. It must be guided by an overarching philosophy and principles and accompanied by a culture of evidence that draws continuous attention to how any changes are affecting the experience and outcomes for students, as well as a sense of purpose and recognition that knowledge must have consequences in order to be meaningful. Given what we know about learning, STEM is especially well suited as a means to promote deeper learning and understanding.

- *Faculty must understand who their students are, their backgrounds and preparation, and their educational goals.* In recent years, many faculty have been taken by surprise by the remarkable changes in the attitudes, motivations, and levels of preparation of students entering college. Good information about who our students are, what they think, what they do with their time, and, for that matter, how much time they have to concentrate on their studies is essential. Otherwise we will prepare a banquet for guests who arrive tired, disinterested, satiated by junk food, and generally unreceptive to what we offer.

- *There must be a supportive environment for curricular change.* A supportive environment has a number of elements, all of which must be present to some degree, although the balance and interaction of these components may vary according to the history, culture, and traditions of particular institutions.

First, faculty roles and responsibilities must be compatible with a major investment of time and energy in curricular reform. Second, the promotion and tenure process should incorporate rigorous standards that can be applied not only to traditional research and creative activity but also to the evaluation of what Ernest Boyer (1990) called "the scholarship of teaching."

Third, faculty must be supported by an effective infrastructure and policies that promote collaboration, provide technical assistance for the introduction of new pedagogical approaches, and encourage the evaluation and dissemination of the results of reform as it is being attempted and not simply after the fact. Fourth, sufficient resources must be provided to validate the priority of curricular reform and to support it. This will require reallocation from other priorities and the use of strategic thinking and budgeting at institutional levels. Finally, a point often overlooked in the challenge of curricular reform, time must be taken to understand the process of change itself and explore what can be done to ensure that reform can be sustained and enhanced on an institution-wide scale.

- *It takes a long time to change a campus culture and to install significant curricular changes.* New approaches to STEM must be aligned with other coordinated efforts to introduce a coherent educational philosophy that guides the design and delivery of the undergraduate curriculum and defines the expectations for the undergraduate experience. Such reform is unlikely to succeed when undertaken on an individual course-by-course basis or without articulation with a broader curricular reform agenda.
- *Undergraduate experiences in STEM for both majors and nonmajors should be approached from the perspective of a liberal arts education.* All undergraduates should have an in-depth exposure to the modes of inquiry and significant theoretical and practical aspects of each domain of the liberal arts. The sciences frequently are approached differently from other fields. In English, a student learns to write while simultaneously studying the work of others. In history, a student learns to work with original materials and to analyze and interpret them in the context of historical reasoning while reading the work of historians. In the sciences and mathematics, however, undergraduates have not, until recently, been encouraged or even allowed to engage in original inquiry until they have mastered a significant body of knowledge developed by others. Reforms that introduce undergraduates to discovery and application early in their education can correct this disparity and ensure that students acquire the capacity for moral and ethical reasoning (open-mindedness, an insistence on evidence and empathy for others), as well as a propensity for lifelong learning.
- *Reform in undergraduate STEM can benefit from a close articulation with both K–12 reform and the reform of graduate education in teacher preparation programs and traditional STEM doctoral programs.* There is a logical relationship between K–12 reform and the redesign of undergraduate science curricula. Both require that faculty members have experience with curricular change and with the introduction of different pedagogical strategies and that they be skilled in collaboration with other faculty on campus and with community partners that can offer off-campus opportunities for original research, such as environmental studies.

Supporting the Enhancement of STEM Education:
A National Perspective

Changes in institutional priorities, values, and behaviors are not entirely self-contained. The values and interests of faculty are shaped not only by their experiences during doctoral study but also by what is presented at national and regional meetings and published in professional society journals. Curricular reform itself can be seriously limited by outsiders: the content and expectations incorporated into science and math standards for K–12 assessments and proficiency levels, advanced placement tests and approaches to college-level work in the high schools, college entrance exams, the Graduate Record Exam, and professional school exams such as the Medical College Admission Test. One colleague of mine refers to these as examples of bugs (that is, curriculum) trapped in amber.

Faculty priorities are also strongly influenced by the priorities and funding strategies of federal science agencies. These priorities are implemented by people whose interests and expectations have been influenced by their own experiences in the professoriat. To explore this issue, I will use my experience at the National Science Foundation since that agency has the most comprehensive portfolio of investments in the nation's overall scientific and engineering capacity, including a historic emphasis on STEM education and its linkage to the strength of the research community.

As a direct reflection of the higher education community to which it is so closely tied, NSF is organized like a large research university with a set of directorates that reflect the core disciplines of science and engineering. In addition, it has a directorate, Education and Human Resources (EHR), that operates somewhat like a college of education. In recent years, a growing emphasis on broadening participation in the programs at NSF has expanded the internal culture to incorporate the experiences of other institutional missions, such as community and technical colleges, K–12 schools, and regional comprehensive institutions and private liberal arts colleges, but the dominant culture is still that of the research university. Much of this expansion has been managed and supported by the EHR directorate, whose programs encompass a broader range of societal educational and cultural priorities. The analogy to a university is fairly accurate in that much time and effort must be devoted to linking the education research, programmatic development, and workforce emphases of EHR to the interests of the other directorates, whose primary missions are to advance the frontiers of the disciplines they support.

Cross-cutting priorities, such as nanoscale science or cyberinfrastructure, that match the national research and development agenda are one avenue to promote an integration of effort and investment across directorates. Other means to encourage collaboration include interactions of the program officers, shared development and sponsorship of the prospectus for new solicitations for proposals and interactions that promote both the integration of research and education, and a joint approach to the development

NEW DIRECTIONS FOR TEACHING AND LEARNING • DOI: 10.1002/tl

of strategies to broaden participation in STEM education and research. These efforts depend, as they do in a campus environment, on the interests, inclinations, and experience of the people who staff the different directorate.

Like its counterparts in academia, the environment at NSF poses challenges to the kinds of integrative efforts that will be required to change how the directorates work together and the rethinking and examination of underlying assumptions that intentionally or unintentionally shape what the agency wishes to support, how it writes its solicitations, how its panels of reviewers evaluate the proposals it receives, and how program officers shape their portfolios of awards and interact with their investigators and the field in general. These are important cultural considerations that will change slowly, just as they are shifting in our colleges and universities. As more program officers, division directors, and senior administrators join NSF with different experiences in STEM research and education, the underlying values and assumptions of the agency will grow to reflect the realities of today's research and educational environment.

Some of NSF's solicitations are beginning to incorporate design elements that reflect a working knowledge of institutional culture and practice and demonstrate an intentional effort to direct institutional attention and resources toward new approaches to educational reform. In the development of the Mathematics and Science Partnerships (2006), for example, NSF built in a different approach to research, program evaluation, and technical assistance across the cohort of funded projects that directs the attention of the investigators to a new range of questions that reflect earlier experiences with large-scale change in both urban and rural environments. Grantees are asked to address a common core of issues and to collect comparable data to permit a more comprehensive approach to program evaluation across sites for learning purposes, not just for program justification. Without going into the details of the solicitations themselves or the design and functions of the partnership national learning network, the point is that in this program, careful attention was given to the realities of institutional environments and working relationships, and the solicitation was shaped to correspond to those realities.

A number of other federal agencies and Washington-based organizations also include undergraduate education in their missions and in their programming. In addition to NSF, an agency that stands out from the other federal agencies because of its status as an independent agency without specific regulatory responsibilities, several other science-based agencies that are mission based—they have responsibility for a particular national agenda and include the Department of Energy, the National Aeronautics and Space Agency, the U.S. Department of Agriculture, and smaller agencies such as the National Oceanic and Atmospheric Administration (NOAA) within the U.S. Department of Commerce—provide support for both high school teachers of science and mathematics and for undergraduates pursuing degrees in STEM fields and their faculty mentors. These efforts are in part designed to ensure that the United States continues to benefit from a strong research base and in part to prepare for the generational transition that will require these agencies to attract a significant number of U.S. citizens to their workforce. To get an idea of the scope of these activities, visit some of the agency Web sites. For example, the NOAA education resources page (http://www.research.noaa.gov/education/) offers a wealth of education resources for educators and leads the reader to opportunities within the agency itself and support for students who are interested in advanced study in the fields represented in NOAA's portfolio. As the Web site explains, "NOAA actively provides students with a variety of opportunities to develop academic excellence and scientific rigor in NOAA's areas of expertise (e.g., ocean and atmospheric science/research, fisheries, satellites, weather, etc.). Many individuals graduating from these education programs continue their professional careers in the sciences and work for NOAA or partner institutions. The collective efforts of these opportunities are aimed at increasing the size and diversity of the pool of future candidates for STEM-related professional positions" (2007).

Although there is not agreement on whether we have a surplus of STEM professionals, an adequate supply, or an impending crisis because of an insufficient number of graduates in these fields, federal mission-based science agencies demonstrate a strong commitment to encouraging promising students to pursue these fields, as researchers or teachers or both, and to supporting those interested with engaging materials that draw students and their instructors into the study of the fields that support these agencies. The NOAA site is fairly typical in its explanation of the rationale for its emphasis on support for advanced study in STEM fields, as well as its educational resources for classroom teachers and students.

To guide these national efforts as well as to support local and regional efforts to address STEM workforce needs, the National Research Council conducts a steady stream of inquiries into a number of aspects of undergraduate STEM education, as well as the preparation of K–12 teachers of science and mathematics and thoughtful studies about such topics as how people learn (Bransford, Brown, and Cocking, 2000), the future of biomedical science education (National Research Council, 2003), and studies and recommendations on a variety of STEM education topics. These documents have become mainstays of the innovation movement within STEM education. Over the past decade, these efforts have also been advanced through the efforts of Project Kaleidoscope with an emphasis on the design of science facilities for campus communities, a study of institutional innovation and change, and a network that supports faculty leadership of change. On its Web site, Project Kaleidoscope (2007) outlines its mission as follows:

> The vision of Project Kaleidoscope (PKAL) is of an environment in which all American undergraduates have access to learning experiences in fields of science, technology, engineering, and mathematics (STEM) that motivate them to persist in their studies and consider careers in these fields.

NEW DIRECTIONS FOR TEACHING AND LEARNING • DOI: 10.1002/tl

Our vision is of a learning environment that brings all undergraduates to an understanding of the influence of science and technology in their world. Based on this vision, PKAL's goal is to call for attention to practices and policies that affect the quality and character of the learning of undergraduates. This includes attention to what works in the process of institutional transformation, to the work of leaders shaping the culture and establishing the human and physical infrastructure supportive of robust student learning.

Finally, within the context of disciplinary and professional societies, a number of important projects and programs have been designed and implemented that are bringing serious purpose and professional recognition to faculty members who elect to pursue the study of how students learn in the context of particular disciplines. These efforts also provide a venue for the presentation of reports and the publication of scholarly work. Most professional organizations now have an education component that is reflected in their meeting structure, professional journals, and work with other societies and agencies. These efforts address a critical need: the provision of scholarly outlets for the scholarship of learning and teaching within the STEM disciplines as well as within the related cognitive and learning sciences.

Conclusion

The stimulation and sense of purpose that is provided by the remarkable advances we are seeing today in the sciences and engineering are beginning to generate new and exciting interdisciplinary fields, new methodologies, and new kinds of questions that we could not even have asked ourselves a few years ago. We cannot define our task as simply to develop strategies for enhancing the undergraduate STEM curriculum. In fact, these goals are on the path to a much more important, much more profound set of goals: to rethink what we mean by an undergraduate education and to use the excitement of the new science as a starting point for engaging students in the greatest intellectual adventure we have ever seen.

References

Atkinson, R. D. *The Past and Future of America's Economy: Long Waves of Innovation and Power Cycles of Growth.* Northampton, Mass.: Elgar Publishing, 2004.
Boyer, E. L. *Scholarship Reconsidered: Priorities of the Professoriate.* Princeton, N.J.: Carnegie Foundation for the Advancement of Teaching, 1990.
Bransford, J. D., Brown, A. L., and Cocking, R. R. *How People Learn: Brain, Mind, Experience and School.* Washington, D.C.: National Academy Press, 2000.
Commission on Work, Family and Citizenship. William T. Grant Foundation. *The Forgotten Half Revisited: American Youth and Young Families, 1998–2008.* (Samuel Halperin, ed.). 1998. Retrieved May 16, 2005, from http://www.wtgrantfoundation. org/index.htm.

Feltovich, P. J., Coulson, R. L., and Spiro, R. J. "Learners' (Mis)Understanding of Important and Difficult Concepts." In K. D. Forbes and P. S. Feltovich (eds.), *Smart Machines in Education: The Coming Revolution in Educational Technology.* Cambridge, Mass.: MIT Press, 2001.

Foray, D. *The Economics of Knowledge.* Cambridge, Mass.: MIT Press, 2004.

Huber, M. T., and Hutchings, P. *Integrative Learning, Mapping the Terrain.* Washington, D.C.: Association of American Colleges and Universities, 2004.

Leskes, A. "Foreword." In M. T. Huber and P. Hutchings, *Integrative Learning: Mapping the Terrain.* Washington, D.C.: Association of American Colleges and Universities, 2004.

Marburger, J. H., and Portman, R. "Memorandum on FY 2008 Administrative Research and Development Budget Priorities." June 23, 2006. Retrieved Dec. 3, 2006, from http://usgeo.gov/docs/OSTP-OMB%20Guidance%20Memo%20for%20FY08.pdf.

National Governors Association. "Innovation America Call to Action and Concept Paper." Washington, D.C.: National Governors Association, 2006.

National Oceanic and Atmospheric Administration. "NOAA's Educational Opportunities for Students." 2007. Retrieved Sept. 24, 2007, from http://www.magazine.noaa.gov/stories/mag201.htm.

National Research Council. *BIO 2010: Transforming Undergraduate Education for Future Research Biologists/Committee on Undergraduate Biology Education to Prepare Research Scientists for the 21st Century. Board of Life Sciences. Division of Earth and Life Sciences.* Washington, D.C.: National Research Council of the National Academies, 2003.

National Science Foundation. "Strategic Plan 2006–2011." 2006. Retrieved Dec. 3, 2006, from http://www.nsf.gov/pubs/2006/nsf0648/nsf0648.jsp.

Office of Science and Technology Policy and Office of Management and Budget. "FY 2008 Administration Research and Development Budget Priorities." Memorandum for the Heads of Executive Departments and Agencies. June 23, 2006. Retrieved Jan. 16, 2009, from http://usgeo.gov/docs/OSTPOMB%20Guidance%20Memo%20for%20FY08.pdf.

Organization for Economic Cooperation and Development. "Policy Brief: The Significance of Knowledge Management in the Business Sector." 2004. Retrieved May 16, 2005, from http://www.oecd.org/dataoecd/53/40/33641372.pdf.

Project Kaleidoscope. "Mission Statement." 2007. Retrieved Sept. 24, 2007, from http://www.pkal.org/.

JUDITH A. RAMALEY *is president of Winona State University and was assistant director of the education and human resources directorate at the National Science Foundation from 2001 to 2004.*

NEW DIRECTIONS FOR TEACHING AND LEARNING • DOI: 10.1002/tl

7

This chapter describes programs created to improve the preparation of future STEM faculty for their roles as educators.

Preparing STEM Doctoral Students for Future Faculty Careers

Ann E. Austin, Henry Campa III, Christine Pfund, Donald L. Gillian-Daniel, Robert Mathieu, Judith Stoddart

One strategy for improving the quality of undergraduate education, with potential impact over decades, involves greater attention to the preparation of doctoral students who will soon fill the faculty ranks. Doctoral education is a time of socialization for future careers, including faculty work. In recognition of the important role of doctoral education in strengthening undergraduate teaching and learning, various efforts are underway to take a strategic and systematic approach to preparing STEM faculty for the future. In this chapter, we explain the role of doctoral education as a socializing process, present common concerns about doctoral education as preparation for faculty work, and briefly survey the range of programs to improve faculty preparation during doctoral education. Then we highlight two programs within the Center for the Integration of Research, Teaching, and Learning (CRTL), sponsored by the National Science Foundation, whose comprehensive nature makes them useful examples of institutional efforts specifically focused on preparing effective STEM faculty for the future.

H. Campa and J. Stoddart acknowledge K. Klomparens, M. Helm, T. Nunez, N. Speer, and M. Urban-Lurain for their insights and assistance with program development and implementation at Michigan State University.

Doctoral Education as Socialization for Faculty Careers

In their recent review of the literature on socialization as it relates to doctoral education, Austin and McDaniels (2006) explained that "socialization is a process of internalizing the expectations, standards, and norms of a given society" (p. 400), which includes learning the relevant skills, knowledge, habits, attitudes, and values of the group that one is joining. After reviewing the work of Weidman, Twale, and Stein (2001) as well as that of a number of other scholars who study socialization, Austin and McDaniels (2006) summarized several key implications pertaining to the socialization of future faculty:

- Prospective faculty need opportunities to invest time in the profession, learn the knowledge and skills used by faculty members, and interact with faculty in ways that help them understand faculty life (Weidman, Twale, and Stein, 2001).
- The socialization process is not simple and linear, but complex and ongoing. It does not happen through just one or two events or opportunities, but rather through many diverse experiences occurring over a time period.
- Many different people influence prospective faculty members, including their peers (an important group in helping them engage in sense making about their experiences), faculty members, colleagues in professional associations, and friends and family.
- The process of socialization is not a one-way process where prospective faculty members are passively influenced by others; rather, socialization involves a dialectical, bidirectional process in which the newcomers are affected by the organization and profession they will join, and bring their own ideas, values, and expectations into the new environment (Tierney and Rhoads, 1994; Tierney and Bensimon, 1996).

These findings from the research provide useful ideas to those developing programs to prepare future faculty.

Although arguably the effective socialization and preparation of prospective faculty is one of the most critically important responsibilities of graduate education, we note four areas of concern pertaining to doctoral students' preparation that have appeared in the research on doctoral education over the past decade (Austin, 2002a, 2002b; Golde and Dore, 2001; Lovitts, 2001; Wulff, Austin, Nyquist, and Sprague, 2004). First, doctoral education does not provide enough systematic preparation for the various roles a faculty member must fulfill, including teaching. While doctoral students often gain research experience by apprenticing with faculty members, they usually learn little about other responsibilities, such as advising, serving on institutional committees, and engaging in outreach that connects scholarly expertise with societal problems. In regard to teaching specifically, many doctoral students have minimal opportunity to develop teaching abilities in thoughtful, systematic ways. In fact, teaching assignments in STEM fields often are regarded as less prestigious than research assignments, tasks to be fulfilled only until the student wins a place on a research team. In addition, teaching assignments are usually made on the basis of institutional need rather than with attention to the professional development needs of the doctoral students (Austin, 2002a, 2002b; Wulff, Austin, Nyquist, and Sprague, 2004). Second, doctoral students sometimes receive conflicting messages about what is important in their careers and where to put emphasis in their preparation. While their institutions may articulate messages about the importance of the teaching mission, their advisors, particularly in STEM fields, may urge them to avoid spending too much time on teaching preparation in order to ensure sufficient attention to research. Third, doctoral students often express concern regarding lack of explicit feedback about their development. While they may aspire to faculty positions, they do not necessarily have regular opportunities to discuss with their advisors their progress in developing relevant abilities, including teaching skills. Fourth, future faculty often have little opportunity in graduate school to learn about the range of available career opportunities, including, for example, working in liberal arts colleges or community colleges, where teaching may be rewarded more heavily than research.

The past decade has seen a number of creative, purposeful responses to these concerns, ranging from inventories of the abilities and skills that doctoral education should help prospective faculty develop to the development, testing, and implementation of various programs to better prepare future faculty. For example, Austin and McDaniels (2006) have laid out a conceptual framework of the abilities and skills appropriate for faculty in the twenty-first century. These include conceptual understanding not only of one's discipline but also of the history of higher education, the types of higher education institutions, and one's professional identity as a scholar and professor; knowledge and skills concerning teaching and learning processes, research, engagement and service, and institutional citizenship; interpersonal skills in regard to communication, collaboration, and working with diverse people; and professional attitudes and habits pertaining to ethics, lifelong learning, cultivating professional networks, and maintaining passion and balance.

National organizations as well as universities have developed promising programmatic efforts to reform doctoral education and improve the preparation of future faculty. For example, the Council of Graduate Schools (CGS) is an active forum in which graduate deans share innovative institutional strategies, programs, and policies. The Association of American Colleges and Universities as well as CGS have supported the Preparing Future Faculty Program, which has developed models for linking universities with liberal arts colleges, comprehensive institutions, and community colleges in order to provide opportunities for doctoral students to explore faculty work while finishing their degrees (Gaff, Pruitt-Logan, and Weibl, 2000; Pruitt-Logan and Gaff, 2004). Beginning in 2001, the Carnegie Foundation for the

Advancement of Teaching facilitated a five-year project, the Carnegie Initiative on the Doctorate; its purpose was to help doctoral programs in six disciplinary areas to strengthen and reform the ways in which they prepared future scholars as "stewards of the discipline" (Walker, 2004).

While these initiatives have addressed preparation of future faculty across a number of disciplines, the National Science Foundation (NSF) has supported a national initiative, the Center for the Integration of Research, Teaching, and Learning (CIRTL), designed to address the particular issues associated with preparing future faculty in the STEM fields. The mission of CIRTL is to develop a national faculty in science, technology, engineering, and mathematics (STEM) with the knowledge and experience to forge successful professional careers that include implementing and advancing effective teaching and learning practices. CIRTL is accomplishing this mission through high-impact professional development in teaching and learning for STEM graduate students and postdoctoral researchers, the future faculty of the nation. As one of NSF's national centers for teaching and learning, CIRTL aims to have a national impact through the collaboration of a set of research universities committed to developing models for preparing STEM faculty who are prepared to excel in teaching as well as research. CIRTL has established three conceptual pillars to guide its work:

- Teaching-As-Research, the deliberate, systematic, and reflective use of research methods by instructors to develop and implement teaching practices that advance the learning experiences and outcomes of both students and teachers.
- Learning Communities, which bring together groups of people for shared learning, discovery, and generation of knowledge. To achieve common learning goals, a learning community nurtures functional relationships among its members.
- Learning-Through-Diversity, which recognizes that excellence and diversity are necessarily intertwined. True learning through diversity capitalizes on the rich array of experiences, backgrounds, and skills among all students to enhance the learning of all.

The University of Wisconsin–Madison, Michigan State University, and the Pennsylvania State University formed the initial network to develop and test CIRTL programs. Other institutional members have recently joined the CIRTL Network, including the University of Colorado at Boulder, Howard University, Texas A&M University, and Vanderbilt University. The remaining sections of this chapter describe the programs in place at two CIRTL Network partners: the University of Wisconsin–Madison, where the initial prototype for CIRTL was designed, and Michigan State University, where a CIRTL program specifically for STEM doctoral students has been developed to build on an existing graduate school program designed to prepare doctoral students for a range of careers. These two programs highlight the work of CIRTL and

NEW DIRECTIONS FOR TEACHING AND LEARNING • DOI: 10.1002/tl

provide examples of institutional efforts to prepare STEM doctoral students as future faculty who will improve undergraduate learning.

University of Wisconsin–Madison's Delta Program in Research, Teaching, and Learning

The Delta Program in Research, Teaching, and Learning at the University of Wisconsin–Madison is the prototype program of CIRTL. A commitment to the conceptual pillars of CIRTL—Teaching-as-Research, Learning Communities, and Learning-Through-Diversity—is woven into the design of every component of the Delta Program. (One-page descriptions as well as frameworks that describe developmental steps of participants as they put these ideas into action can be found at www.cirtl.net.) We have found that a learning community of graduate students, postdoctoral researchers, academic staff, and faculty (graduates-through-faculty) built on these three ideas is an effective approach to improving preparation for teaching, enhancing student learning, and promoting institutional change (Connolly, Bouwma-Gearhart, and Clifford, 2007; Brower, Carlson-Dakes, and Bargar, 2007).

The core of the Delta Program is a curriculum of graduate courses, intergenerational small-group programs, and internships embedded within an interdisciplinary learning community. Delta also offers a small number of targeted workshops and hosts monthly roundtable dinners. A certificate recognizes participant accomplishments within the Delta Program.

Every facet of Delta is designed around a research model familiar to STEM graduate students, postdocs, and faculty. Delta courses are project based and require students to define a learning problem, understand their student audience, explore the literature for prior knowledge, hypothesize, design and implement a solution, acquire and analyze data to measure learning outcomes, and revise their materials and approach based on their findings. Delta internships are research assistantships in teaching, in which a graduate student or postdoc partners with a faculty or academic staff member to address a learning problem. Delta activities are designed to provide each graduate student and postdoc participant with a portfolio, letters of recommendation, and presentations or publications in teaching and learning analogous to those in their disciplinary curriculum vitae. Finally, each Delta course and program is taught by a research-active STEM faculty member in partnership with faculty from the social sciences. Such pairings provide powerful combinations of experience, theoretical foundation, and role modeling for future STEM faculty.

Evidence of Success. Evaluation data that are collected across the program about participation, satisfaction, learning, application, and impact provide clear evidence of the success of Delta's approach for future faculty professional development in teaching and learning. From September 2003 through December 2007, over fourteen hundred STEM graduates-through-faculty engaged in the Delta Program. In an average semester, over one hundred graduates-through-faculty take part in semester-long courses and programs, and an additional 150 to 250 participate in roundtable dinners and workshops. In the 2006–2007 academic year, 60 percent of reporting participants were graduate students, 6 percent postdocs, 16 percent faculty, and 20 percent academic staff. The Delta learning community is also highly interdisciplinary: 25 percent physical and mathematical sciences, 36 percent biological sciences, 16 percent engineering sciences, and 13 percent social, behavioral, and economic sciences.

Satisfaction results from across the entire program are very high. For example, 95 percent of participants involved in courses, small-group programs, and internships during fall 2005 reported being satisfied or extremely satisfied with their experiences. In addition, 44 percent of the graduate student participants to date have engaged in fifteen or more hours of Delta programming, the equivalent of more than a semester-long course. Since summer 2004, sixty-five Delta interns have designed, implemented, and analyzed projects to address student learning challenges at University of Wisconsin–Madison or nearby colleges. These represent major commitments and are arguably the most significant measure of satisfaction for an already busy graduate student population.

The vitality of an interdisciplinary and intergenerational learning community is essential to the impact and growth of Delta, and much thought and energy have been put into fostering functional and social connections between members of the community. For example, at the programmatic level, we try to connect program participants with our monthly roundtable dinners. Those who attend the dinners are then asked to bring what they learned back to the discussions in their courses and programs the following week. Evidence for the strength of the learning community includes a strong sense of identification with Delta among participants, development of a common language and practice, continued and ongoing participation in program activities, programmatic leadership and instruction, and creation of new opportunities by learning community members for both the learning community and the campus (Brower, Carlson-Dakes, and Bargar, 2007). Interestingly, many participants of the Delta Program who have graduated from University of Wisconsin–Madison and moved on to postdoctoral or faculty positions remain connected to the learning community.

The Learning-Through-Diversity concept has sparked and guided many efforts within and beyond the Delta Program. For example, the Delta Program both facilitates semester-long Expeditions in Learning, small groups of STEM graduates-through-faculty that explore the implementation of Learning-Through-Diversity ideas across the campus, and offers a graduate course, Diversity in the College Classroom (Pawley, Pfund, Miller Lauffer, and Handelsman, 2006). Importantly, Delta is focused on initiatives that move learning community members from awareness and reflection to putting the Learning-Through-Diversity concept into action in their teaching.

As a foundation for such Learning-Through-Diversity initiatives, CIRTL developed the CIRTL Diversity Resources (http://www.cirtl.net/Diversity

Institute), which foster discussions about teaching to diverse student audiences, initiate improvements in teaching practice, and improve classroom climate and course content. These resources include a research-literature review that describes inclusive teaching practices and their impact on students in STEM-friendly language, a case book of provocative and challenging diversity-related STEM teaching situations, a resource book that assists STEM instructors in teaching inclusively throughout their courses, and a collection of syllabi from courses that integrate diversity awareness with STEM content. The CIRTL Diversity Resources are integrated into Delta course and program materials and activities. In addition, they are now more broadly used in the annual University of Wisconsin Teaching Academy Summer Institute for faculty and into teaching assistant training in the College of Engineering and the Department of Chemistry. A study group at the Nelson Institute for Environmental Studies uses the diversity case studies as a foundation for their discussions on diversity in their discipline. University of Wisconsin STEM faculty and staff in biology, chemistry, engineering, physics, mathematics, and plant pathology have begun to use the Diversity Resources in undergraduate and graduate STEM courses to help engage students in discussion of diversity and to use that diversity to enhance the learning of everyone in those courses.

The ultimate measure of Delta's success must be measured by the future teaching practices of participants and by their teaching-as-research to establish the learning of their students. To this end, an interview-based longitudinal study, launched in 2005, is following eighty-five graduate students and postdocs who participated at varying levels in Delta (and other future faculty development programs in some cases) as they finish and move into their first professional positions. The 2005 and 2006 interview data show that participation resulted in attainment of valued new knowledge and skills about teaching, positive changes in attitudes toward teaching, and expanded views of the types of academic roles they might play and types of institutions of interest to them for their careers. Those graduate students and postdocs who have moved into first positions report that their experiences in programs such as Delta helped them adjust effectively and creatively to the teaching-related demands of their new positions (Bouwma-Gearhart, Bargar, Millar, and Connolly 2007).

Impacts of the Delta Program. The impacts of the Delta Program go beyond the participants themselves. For example, each Delta intern has an impact on student learning in a wide array of STEM courses. Moreover, the instructional approaches and materials developed are incorporated in the standard teaching practices of these courses and the departments in which they are taught. Most broadly, they are shared through campus presentations to other instructors and nationally through publications and presentations at disciplinary meetings (D'Amato and others, 2007; Kerr and Walz, 2007). The CIRTL Network also provides a natural dissemination route for these instructional innovations. Ultimately Delta participants go on to careers at other institutions and take with them the skills and abilities to improve student learning throughout their careers.

At the institutional level, the Delta Program enhances both the research mission and the teaching mission of the campus. For example, Delta provides faculty with the capacity to address the broader impact funding criteria of federal agencies like NSF. Over half of the 2006 and 2007 NSF faculty early career development (CAREER) award recipients at the University of Wisconsin–Madison incorporated Delta into their proposals in order to accomplish their educational plans. Proposal reviewers frequently commented favorably on their plans to partner with Delta to achieve broader impacts. In addition, Delta is increasing the ability of the University of Wisconsin–Madison to recruit the best graduate students. Ultimately the impact of Delta on the university is perhaps best recognized by the fact that the Delta Program is now fully institutionalized, operating entirely on university funding. Moreover, members of the learning community continue to volunteer their energy, leadership, and time to support the advancement and growth of the Delta Program at the University of Wisconsin–Madison.

Michigan State University's Professional Development Model

The CIRTL Program at Michigan State University (MSU) builds on an innovative and well-conceptualized professional development program offered through the graduate school to doctoral students across disciplines. The career and professional development model developed by the graduate school focuses on a multistage approach to navigating the doctoral experience and making the transition to a faculty position. Known by the acronym PREP, the model foregrounds four professional skills that are key to a successful graduate and professional career: **P**lanning throughout the graduate program to identify and achieve career goals, developing **R**esilience and tenacity to thrive through personal and professional stages, practicing active **E**ngagement in making important life decisions and in acquiring the skills necessary to attain career goals, and attaining high standards of **P**rofessionalism in research, teaching, and service. The goals of the PREP program are to promote graduate student retention and completion, enhance professional development opportunities in graduate school, give students a competitive edge securing professional positions, and supplement departmental advising activities.

Under the PREP model, workshops are tailored to target the four skills at three stages of a graduate program: early (course work, qualifying exams, research design and dissertation prospectus, career planning), mid (certifying exams, research implementation, developing professional networks), and late (dissertation writing, job search, postdoc or other postgraduate job opportunities in agencies or industry). Partners from the graduate school, career services, the office of the vice president for research and graduate studies, and the teaching assistant program collaborate to plan a coordinated set of career workshops and conferences that move students through the PREP professional development model.

This common focus allows the graduate school to conduct coordinated evaluations of each program and design long-term research projects on the impacts of such interventions on doctoral completion and the transition to faculty life. The evaluation effort will also create partnerships among offices across campus, forging a coordinated focus on doctoral student development that is unique in the national landscape of large public research universities. The PREP model not only serves graduate students; it also strengthens the overall infrastructure for doctoral education at MSU.

The organizational tool for the PREP programs is a matrix (for a fully interactive version, go to http://grad.msu.edu/cpd.htm) that offers a gateway to career and professional development resources at MSU (Table 7.1).

On the Web site, each cell of the PREP matrix is an interactive link that leads to discussion of specific strategies (for example, skills and workshops) for addressing the career and professional needs relevant to the stage of graduate education highlighted in the particular cell.

The PREP model responds to the recent research on graduate student development discussed earlier in this chapter—from studies that have investigated the gap between the graduate school experience and the first years in an academic or nonacademic position (Golde and Dore, 2001; Nyquist,

Table 7.1. The PREP Matrix of MSU Workshops and Programs: Professional Thematic Areas

Stage	Planning	Resilience	Engagement	Professionalism
Early	The PREP'd Ph.D.	Navigating the Ph.D.: A Writing Workshop	From Student to Professor: Stages of Professional Development	Responsible Conduct of Research
Mid	Networking for Ph.D.s Identifying Nonacademic Options The Academic Job Search	Conflict Resolution Dissertation Writing Workshops	Translating Academic Success into Expanded Career Opportunities	Responsible Conduct of Research Certification in College Teaching Teaching Assistant Program Workshops
Late	Dissertation Formatting CV and Interviewing Skills Workshops	Conflict Resolution	Securing Positions at Two- and Four-Year Institutions FAST Fellowship Program	CASTL Fellowship Program Hans Kende Memorial Lecture Series

NEW DIRECTIONS FOR TEACHING AND LEARNING • DOI: 10.1002/tl

Austin, Sprague, and Wulff, 2001; Nerad and Cerny, 1999) to those that consider factors contributing to completion and attrition (Council of Graduate Schools, 2004; Lovitts, 2001; Weidman, Twale, and Stein, 2001; Golde, 2000; Tinto, 1993). Information gathered in the spring 2007 MSU Graduate Student Survey is being used to refine this professional development program so that it better meets the changing needs of graduate students for academic and nonacademic career opportunities. Under the auspices of a Council of Graduate School Ph.D. Completion Project Grant, the graduate school is also studying to what extent professional development models are dependent on disciplinary structures of knowledge.

Preliminary Evidence of Success and Early Impacts of PREP. Interest in PREP offerings is growing. In the 2006–2007 academic year, this series attracted 376 graduate students from across disciplines for sessions on topics such as engaging in ongoing professional development, interviewing for and thriving in academic positions at two- and four-year institutions, and translating doctoral skills into successful positions in federal agencies, nonprofits, industry, and academic administration. In these all-day-Saturday miniconferences, students interacted with national leaders in industry, agencies, nongovernment organizations, and academe, and they developed practical professional skills through interactive breakout sessions.

Feedback from graduate students attending the miniconferences indicates that the relatively short (one-day) professional development intervention provides critical information to students and may influence how they prepare for their future careers. For example, in the "Professionalism and Professional Development in the Academy" program, students' understanding of institutional expectations for faculty to attain tenure significantly increased as a result of the materials presenters shared during the program. Students also reported having a significantly greater understanding of the diversity of skills required at academic institutions to be effective teachers. When workshop participants were asked in a postworkshop survey how they would alter the way they approach their professional development, several themes emerged. Most notably, students were going to be more proactive and aggressive to take advantage of professional development activities while in graduate school, keep a portfolio of their professional development activities, and be more systematic and intentional about planning for their professional development needs. Long-term evaluations will look at the effect on career development planning and timely completion of the doctoral program. Few national studies have addressed how we know whether specific interventions make a difference in graduate education. PREP attempts to establish parameters for such a discussion.

The FAST Fellowship Program: A Component of PREP to Prepare the Next Generation of Science Educators. As part of MSU's involvement in CIRTL, the graduate school sponsors the FAST Fellowship Program (*Future Academic Scholars in Teaching*) specifically for doctoral students in STEM fields. The primary goals of the FAST program are to provide opportunities for a diverse group of Ph.D. students in natural sciences, agriculture and natural resources, engineering, and veterinary medicine to have mentored teaching experiences and gain familiarity with materials on teaching, learning, and assessment techniques. This program was also developed in response to the national need in the sciences to prepare future faculty for the changing needs and expectations in higher education. Students selected for this one-year program participate in group meetings and workshops with fellowship recipients, outside speakers, and faculty members to discuss topics related to teaching and learning. Fellowship recipients propose and conduct a scholarly project on a topic they select regarding doing teaching-as-research. Assistance with projects is provided by a mentor, selected by each fellow and fellowship steering committee members. Fellows are encouraged and supported to disseminate project results on Web sites, at conferences, and in peer-reviewed journals. Each fellow receives a thousand dollars to help support project expenses and travel to a conference to disseminate findings.

The intent of this program is to provide Ph.D. students with a stronger foundation in which to teach as well as to assess the impacts of their teaching on learning. To assess the relative impacts of this program on the students' understanding of teaching and learning concepts and applications to conduct research on their teaching, fellowship recipients complete a Web-based survey at the start of the program and after completion. The program is only in its second year, but program leaders hope that long-term evaluation results will show that the program provides fellows with a fast start to successful and satisfying academic careers in the STEM fields.

Conclusion

Improving undergraduate education in STEM fields will require not only the commitment of the current faculty but also the thorough preparation of the next generation of faculty in ways that lead them to value teaching and to have the knowledge and skills to excel in this aspect of their work. As research on doctoral education indicates, graduate education has typically not prepared the future professoriat as effectively as needed for the responsibilities they must assume as teachers and faculty. The CIRTL Network is developing a variety of effective institutional programs and strategies specifically designed to help STEM doctoral students learn to use their research skills to improve their teaching and their students' learning. In the next three years, in addition to the institutional programs already in place or currently in design, the CIRTL Network will be developing cross-institutional programs that address the same purpose. The next generation of faculty should be ready to be strategic, committed, and creative in their efforts to improve undergraduate student learning in the STEM fields.

NEW DIRECTIONS FOR TEACHING AND LEARNING • DOI: 10.1002/tl

References

Austin, A. E. "Creating a Bridge to the Future: Preparing New Faculty to Face Changing Expectations in a Shifting Context." *Review of Higher Education*, 2002a, 26(2), 119–144.

Austin, A. E. "Preparing the Next Generation of Faculty: Graduate School as Socialization to the Academic Career." *Journal of Higher Education*, 2002b, 73(1), 94–122.

Austin, A. E., and McDaniels, M. "Preparing the Professoriate of the Future: Graduate Student Socialization for Faculty Roles." In J. C. Smart (ed.), *Handbook of Theory and Research*. New York: Springer, 2006.

Bouwma-Gearhart, J., Barger, S., Millar, S., and Connolly, M. "Doctoral and Postdoctoral STEM Teaching-Related Professional Development: Effects on Training and Early Career Periods." WCER working paper 2007–8. 2007. Retrieved Jan. 11, 2009, from http://www.wcer.wisc.edu/publications/workingPapers/Working_Paper_No_2007_08.pdf.

Brower, A. M., Carlson-Dakes, C. G., and Bargar, S. S. "A Learning Community Model of Graduate Student Professional Development for Teaching Excellence." WISCAPE Occasional Paper Series. 2007. Retrieved Jan. 11, 2009, from http://www.wiscape.wisc.edu/publications/attachments/WP010.pdf.

Connolly, M. R., Bouwma-Gearhart, J. L., and Clifford, M. A. "The Birth of a Notion: The Windfalls and Pitfalls of Tailoring an SOTL-like Concept to Scientists, Mathematicians and Engineering." *Innovative Higher Education*, 2007, 32(1), 19–34.

Council of Graduate Schools. "Ph.D. Completion and Attrition: Policy, Numbers, Leadership, and Next Steps." Washington, D.C.: Council of Graduate Schools, 2004.

D'Amato, M. J., and others. "Introducing New Learning Tools into a Standard Classroom: A Multi-Tool Approach to Integrating Fuel-Cell Concepts into Introductory College Chemistry." *Journal of Chemical Education*, 2007, 84(2), 248–252.

Golde, C. M. "Should I Stay or Should I Go? Student Descriptions of the Doctoral Attrition Process." *Review of Higher Education*, 2000, 3(2), 1999–227.

Golde, C. M., and Dore, T. M. *At Cross Purposes: What the Experiences of Today's Doctoral Students Reveal About Doctoral Education*. Philadelphia: Pew Charitable Trusts, 2001.

Kerr, S., and Walz, K. "'Holes' in Student Understanding: Addressing Prevalent Misconceptions Regarding Atmospheric Environmental Chemistry." *Journal of Chemical Education*, 2007, 84(10), 1693–1696.

Lovitts, B. E. *Leaving the Ivory Tower: The Causes and Consequences of Departure from Doctoral Study*. Lanham, Md.: Rowman and Littlefield, 2001.

Nerad, M., and Cerny, J. "From Rumors to Facts: Career Outcomes of English Ph.D.s." *Council of Graduate Schools Communicator*, 1999, 32(7), 1–11.

Nyquist, J. D., Austin, A. E., Sprague, J., and Wulff, D. H. *The Development of Graduate Students as Teaching Scholars: A Four-Year Longitudinal Study*. Seattle: University of Washington, 2001.

Pawley, A., Pfund, C., Miller Lauffer, S., and Handelsman, J. *A Case Study of "Diversity in the College Classroom," A Course to Improve the Next Generation of Faculty*. Proceedings of the 2006 American Society for Engineering Education Annual Conference and Exposition. Washington, D.C.: American Society for Engineering Education, 2006.

Pruitt-Logan, A. S., and Gaff, J. G. "Preparing Future Faculty: Changing the Culture of Doctoral Education." In D. H. Wulff and A. E. Austin (eds.), *Paths to the Professoriate: Strategies for Enriching the Preparation of Future Faculty*. San Francisco: Jossey-Bass, 2004.

Tierney, W. G., and Bensimon, E. M. *Promotion and Tenure: Community and Socialization in Academe*. Albany: State University of New York Press, 1996.

Tierney, W. G., and Rhoads, R. A. *Enhancing Promotion, Tenure and Beyond: Faculty Socialization as a Cultural Process*. ASHE-ERIC Higher Education Report No. 6. Washington, D.C.: George Washington University, School of Education and Human Development, 1994.

Tinto, V. *Leaving College: Rethinking the Causes and Cures of Student Attrition.* Chicago: University of Chicago Press, 1993.

Walker, G. "The Carnegie Initiative on the Doctorate: Creating Stewards of the Discipline." In D. H. Wulff and A. E. Austin (eds.), *Paths to the Professoriate: Strategies for Enriching the Preparation of Future Faculty.* San Francisco: Jossey-Bass, 2004.

Weidman, J. C., Twale, J. J., and Stein, E. L. *Socialization of Graduate and Professional Students in Higher Education: A Perilous Passage?* ASHE-ERIC Higher Education Report Vol. 28, No. 3. San Francisco: Jossey-Bass, 2001.

Wulff, D. H., Austin, A. E., Nyquist, J. D., and Sprague, J. "The Development of Graduate Students as Teaching Scholars: A Four-Year Longitudinal Study." In D. H. Wulff and A. E. Austin (eds.), *Paths to the Professoriate: Strategies for Enriching the Preparation of Future Faculty.* San Francisco: Jossey-Bass, 2004.

ANN E. AUSTIN *is co–principal investigator of CIRTL and Mildred B. Erickson Professor of Higher, Adult, and Lifelong Education at Michigan State University.*

HENRY CAMPA III *is professor of fisheries and wildlife and assistant dean of the Graduate School at Michigan State University.*

CHRISTINE PFUND *is associate director of the Delta Program in Research, Teaching, and Learning and the codirector of the Wisconsin Program for Scientific Teaching at the University of Wisconsin–Madison.*

DONALD L. GILLIAN-DANIEL *is associate director of the Delta Program in Research, Teaching, and Learning at the University of Wisconsin–Madison.*

ROBERT MATHIEU *is director and principal investigator of CIRTL and professor of astronomy at the University of Wisconsin–Madison.*

JUDITH STODDART *is associate professor of English and assistant dean of the Graduate School at Michigan State University.*

NEW DIRECTIONS FOR TEACHING AND LEARNING • DOI: 10.1002/tl

8

Lasting reform of STEM undergraduate education must engage stakeholders from the individual classroom and laboratory to the national policy level.

Climate Change: Creating Conditions Conducive to Quality STEM Undergraduate Education

Roger G. Baldwin

In an era of global competition and a technology-based economy, it is increasingly important that college students graduate with a solid foundation of knowledge and understanding of science and mathematics. They must be able to use their scientific knowledge on their jobs and in their role as citizens of a society where complex policy and resource questions, for example, on cloning, stem cell research, greenhouse gases, and sustainability, increasingly have dimensions related to science and technology.

Systemic Action Needed

Two clear conclusions emerge from this volume. In order to create a climate that supports undergraduate teaching and learning in STEM (science, technology, engineering, and mathematics) fields, the task must be addressed at multiple levels by all of the stakeholders concerned about the quality of STEM undergraduate education. If we wish to change the culture in STEM disciplines in order to promote good teaching in STEM fields, the challenge must be addressed at all levels, from the individual classroom, to discipline-based departments, to college and university curriculum committees. It must be a priority for college and university leaders, leaders of STEM disciplinary societies, and leaders in government as well. Each has a role to play

NEW DIRECTIONS FOR TEACHING AND LEARNING, no. 117, Spring 2009 © Wiley Periodicals, Inc.
Published online in Wiley InterScience (www.interscience.wiley.com) • DOI: 10.1002/tl.347

in the complex process of improving and enhancing the climate that supports undergraduate STEM education

Second, these stakeholders need to coordinate their efforts to maximize their impact. STEM reforms have been advocated at least since the time of *Sputnik,* and piecemeal reforms have been implemented at many institutions. Many of these reforms have stimulated interest in improving STEM undergraduate education and often created positive change. However, in most cases, the impact of these reforms has not been widespread or long lasting. Elaine Seymour (2007) of the University of Colorado reports that "the U.S. STEM education reform effort has lacked mechanisms for coherent and sustained action to build what has been learned and created [to enhance STEM undergraduate education] into nationally-applied strategies." Building a climate that truly supports STEM undergraduate education is much more likely to occur if the key stakeholders coordinate their efforts, communicate, share information and resources, and speak with a unified voice about the importance of reforming undergraduate education in STEM. In other words, we need to address this challenge systemically.

The situation with STEM undergraduate education somewhat parallels that with intercollegiate athletics at American universities. Everyone agrees that the existing system has major flaws and diminishes the collegiate experience of many undergraduates, but no single institution or athletic conference is powerful enough to impose lasting and widespread change. Similarly, no individual STEM reformer, single institution, or STEM discipline working alone is likely to change the culture that puts undergraduate STEM education lower than it should be on a faculty member's list of professional priorities. In contrast, a coalition or alliance of institutions, disciplinary societies, foundations, key government agencies such as the National Science Foundation, and STEM and governmental leaders working together could focus attention, energy, and resources on STEM education and the climate that devalues the education of undergraduates in STEM fields.

Elements of a Reform-Friendly Climate

This volume does not offer a comprehensive strategy for enhancing the climate for undergraduate education in STEM. That task is well beyond its scope. However, each of the chapters addresses an important element of what should be a systematic, coordinated strategy to strengthen STEM undergraduate teaching and learning.

Chapter One uses a meterology metaphor to assess the climate for improving teaching and learning in STEM fields. Baldwin draws from respected national reports to clarify the current status of undergraduate teaching in STEM. He discusses the forces promoting change in STEM undergraduate education and the counterbalancing barriers to substantive and lasting reform. This chapter provides a context for each of the chapters that follow. Smith, Douglas, and Cox show in Chapter Two how educators at the classroom and curriculum levels can apply principles and models of effective educational practice to enhance the learning experience of their students. By carefully designing educational experiences, using active and collaborative learning methods conscientiously, and assessing educational outcomes systematically, STEM professors can create a climate within their classrooms and laboratories that promote student engagement and learning. Improving the climate for learning in STEM undergraduate classes is perhaps the most important step necessary to enhance the overall climate for improved undergraduate education in STEM disciplines.

The teaching groups Coppola advocates in Chapter Three represent another strategy to enhance the climate for improvements in STEM undergraduate education. By forming research-based teaching groups to investigate teaching problems, Coppola acknowledges the dominance of the research culture in most STEM disciplines, and he harnesses that priority in order to improve STEM education. Research-intensive teaching groups do not overturn STEM priorities. Rather, they acknowledge those priorities and use that same inclination to improve practice in STEM education by investigating educational problems in their classrooms and laboratories.

The beauty of Coppola's proposal is that the teaching group can also be a powerful means to induct graduate students and postdocs into a culture that values both research and teaching and develops the attitudes and skills required to enhance both faculty roles. The teaching group can also be a potent means to promote teaching improvement within departments by engaging multiple players from across two or more academic generations in research on teaching concerns.

Certainly enhancing the climate for undergraduate STEM education is not solely a faculty concern or responsibility. Litzinger, Koubek, and Wormley show in Chapter Four that a carefully managed team effort involving faculty and administrators is needed to bring STEM educational improvements to fruition. The authors clarify specifically what administrators can attend to in order to foster a climate conducive to enhanced STEM undergraduate education. These include providing strong leadership in support of reforms, engaging all important stakeholders as reforms are planned, and providing the resources and incentives necessary for educational improvements to be implemented and sustained.

Reform in STEM undergraduate education must accommodate the differences that distinguish one STEM field from another. Certainly efforts to improve the climate for teaching and learning in STEM must be consistent with the culture and distinctive methods of individual disciplines. In Chapter Five, Ferrini-Mundy and Güçler show how several STEM fields have gone about improving educational practice in their own special way. However, they also show that STEM fields use common strategies—active and collaborative learning methods, for example—to improve undergraduate education. Both these similarities and differences suggest that STEM fields have much to gain from communication, and perhaps even some collaboration, with each other as they work toward the shared goal of building a healthy climate for teaching and learning in STEM.

In Chapter Six, Ramaley broadens the perspective on STEM undergraduate education by relating it to dramatic changes in science itself, as well as national concerns about global competitiveness. By looking at the climate for improving undergraduate STEM education from a higher altitude, instead of from the perspective of a single classroom or single college curriculum, it becomes clear how important the job of strengthening STEM education is and how large a task it really is. It is obvious from Ramaley's expansive analysis that many players at the national level (such as the National Science Foundation, the National Research Council, and disciplinary societies) also have a major role to play in creating conditions favorable to STEM education reform. The case Ramaley builds strengthens the argument for a more coordinated effort on behalf of STEM reform than has occurred heretofore. Piecemeal action at many levels may create pockets of improved practice in STEM undergraduate education. However, it is unlikely to raise the overall quality of STEM education to the level necessary to enhance America's competitive edge in a global economy.

Ultimately the campaign to improve STEM undergraduate education will depend on the actions of future generations of STEM professors in colleges and universities. Hence, systematic efforts to prepare aspiring STEM professors for their roles as educators is a key part of the formula for enhancing the climate for improvements in STEM education. When large numbers of future STEM educators are carefully socialized to their roles as teachers and develop the attitudes and skills of effective educators, they will greatly enhance the quality of STEM undergraduate teaching and learning. Austin and her colleagues demonstrate in Chapter Seven the need for institutional and interinstitutional efforts to educate future STEM college and university professors for teaching roles. More important, they profile major programs at research universities that are carefully expanding the nature of STEM graduate education to provide comprehensive preparation for instructional as well as research roles. The University of Wisconsin and Michigan State University programs that the authors review provide instructive models of good practice that other universities can study and adapt to best serve their STEM graduate students who wish to teach in postsecondary education, especially at the undergraduate level.

Conclusion

Quality STEM education has never been more important to the well-being of American society. At the same time, powerful forces remain in place that impede well-meaning efforts to enhance the quality of STEM undergraduate education and make it more welcoming to a broad spectrum of U.S. college students. STEM education reform has been slow and haphazard because the climate or environment for improving STEM education has been indifferent, if not hostile. This volume identifies important actions that can greatly enhance the climate for strengthening STEM undergraduate education. Key actions in support of quality STEM undergraduate education must take place at all levels of our educational system. Supportive actions must also come from relevant government agencies and professional societies that serve the STEM disciplines. Finally, key leaders in and outside higher education must rally against the forces of inertia and work to implement potent incentives for change in STEM undergraduate education.

Improving the climate for the reform of STEM undergraduate education requires rethinking the policies that perpetuate the status quo in STEM classrooms and laboratories, such as requirements for tenure, promotion, and merit pay. It requires an investment or redistribution of resources to raise the priority of STEM undergraduate education on the list of professors' priorities. It requires new faculty development initiatives. We need faculty development programs that adequately prepare future STEM faculty for their very important roles as teachers as well as researchers. We also need programs that help veteran professors stay abreast of the literature on teaching and learning and advances in instructional technology so they can adapt their instruction, enhance learning, and create welcoming and effective educational environments for diverse students. It requires leadership at all levels of the system that sustains and depends on the educational system that prepares scientists, mathematicians, and technology specialists. Systemwide action is necessary to prepare undergraduates who can serve our society by developing technological innovations, supporting economic development, and enhancing living standards in our country.

This volume presents important elements of an environment that would be conducive to improving STEM education at the undergraduate level. It will take a carefully coordinated effort to link the actions recommended here and create an environment that promotes quality STEM education adequate to the demands of a world where science and technology shape the quality of our lives and set our path into the future.

Reference

Seymour, E. "The US Experience of Reform in Science, Technology, Engineering, and Mathematics (STEM) Undergraduate Education." Paper presented to Policies and Practices for Academic Enquiry: An International Colloquium," Winchester, U.K., Apr. 19–21, 2007.

ROGER G. BALDWIN *is professor of educational administration and coordinator of the Higher, Adult, and Lifelong Education Graduate Program at Michigan State University.*

NEW DIRECTIONS FOR TEACHING AND LEARNING • DOI: 10.1002/tl

INDEX

Why Wait to Make Great Discoveries

When you can make them in an instant with
Wiley InterScience® Pay-Per-View and ArticleSelect™

Now you can have instant, full-text access to an extensive collection of journal articles or book chapters available on Wiley InterScience. With Pay-Per-View and ArticleSelect™, there's no limit to what you can discover...

ArticleSelect™ is a token-based service, providing access to full-text content from non-subscribed journals to existing institutional customers (EAL and BAL)

Pay-per-view is available to any user, regardless of whether they hold a subscription with Wiley InterScience.

Benefits:

• Access online full-text content from journals and books that are outside your current library holdings
• Use it at home, on the road, from anywhere at any time
• Build an archive of articles and chapters targeted for your unique research needs
• Take advantage of our free profiled alerting service the perfect companion to help you find specific articles in your field as soon as they're published
• Get what you need instantly no waiting for document delivery
• Fast, easy, and secure online credit card processing for pay-per-view downloads
• Special, cost-savings for EAL customers: whenever a customer spends tokens on a title equaling 115% of its subscription price, the customer is auto-subscribed for the year
• Access is instant and available for 24 hours

WILEY
InterScience®
DISCOVER SOMETHING GREAT

www.interscience.wiley.com

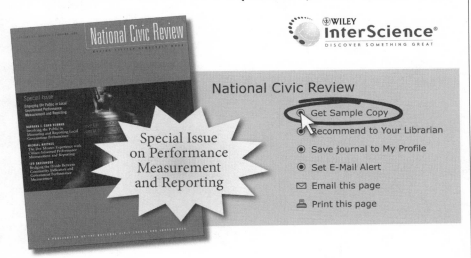